Hounds of the Lord

Other books by Kevin Vost
from Sophia Institute Press:

Memorize the Faith!
Unearthing Your Ten Talents
Fit for Eternal Life!
The One-Minute Aquinas
The Seven Deadly Sins

KEVIN VOST, PSY.D.

HOUNDS

OF THE

LORD

GREAT DOMINICAN
SAINTS EVERY CATHOLIC
SHOULD KNOW

SOPHIA INSTITUTE PRESS
Manchester, New Hampshire

Except where otherwise noted, biblical references in this book are from the Second Catholic Edition of the Revised Standard Version of the Bible (RSV), copyright © 1965, 1966, and 2006 by the Division of Christian Education of the National Council of the Churches of Christ in the United States of America. Used by permission. All rights reserved.

Excerpts from the *Catechism of the Catholic Church*, Second Edition, for use in the United States of America, copyright © 1994 and 1997, United States Catholic Conference — Libreria Editrice Vaticana. Used by permission. All rights reserved.

Sophia Institute Press
Box 5284, Manchester, NH 03108
1-800-888-9344

www.SophiaInstitute.com

Sophia Institute Press® is a registered trademark of Sophia Institute.

Library of Congress Cataloging-in-Publication Data
Vost, Kevin.
    Hounds of the Lord : great Dominican saints every Catholic should know / Kevin Vost, Psy.D.
        pages cm
    Includes bibliographical references.
    ISBN 978-1-62282-289-8 (pbk. : alk. paper) 1. Dominicans — Biography. 2. Christian saints — Biography. I. Title.
    BX3555.V67 2015
    271'.2022 — dc23
    [B]
                                                            2015032981

First printing

To all the religious and lay sons and daughters
of the family of Saint Dominic in our world today,
for the joyful way you embrace the mission of the
Order of Friars Preachers — praising, blessing, and
preaching for the benefit of us all, unto the ends
of the earth, as we journey toward heaven

CONTENTS

PART 3

DOMINICAN LOVERS AND THE CHARITABLE STYLE

Foreword

Jubilees and anniversaries are a great time to reminisce about family, family stories, and individual family members. As the Dominican Order celebrates the eight hundredth anniversary of the approval of the order, we are indebted to Dr. Kevin Vost for providing us with a fresh look at an album of some of these great individuals within the Dominican family.

Reading *St. Albert the Great: Champion of Faith of Reason,* I wondered what the author's connection was with the Dominican Order. He wrote like a Dominican and had unusual insights into the Dominicans, yet there was no "O.P." after his name, but rather a "Psy.D." To quote the Scriptures, "Where then did this man get all this?" (Matt. 13:56).

I had the opportunity to ask that question when Dr. Vost visited Aquinas College. His familial understanding of the Dominicans (and all things Dominican) was handed on to him during the course of his education in the Dominican tradition at both the elementary and high school levels. Having been educated in the riches of the Dominican family, Kevin deftly demonstrates the richness of our Dominican tradition with a stunning variety of saints and blesseds. *Hounds of the Lord* makes clear the lighthearted Dominican adage: "When you've met one Dominican, you've met one Dominican!"

When one thinks of Dominicans, one usually thinks of their great intellects. Kevin Vost, however, provides us with a rich mosaic of the Dominicans that illustrates how these great intellectuals were not simply thinkers. They were (and are!) men and women of love and action as well. Within these pages, there are great preachers, teachers, artists, mystics, nurses, doctors, and even a college student beatified in 1990 by Saint John Paul II.

What do they all have in common? Saint Dominic is the obvious answer, but all the Dominicans in this book, like their founder, brought the message of the gospel, the message of God's mercy, to the people of their time—and the people of our time—by way of example. Kevin Vost shows us the impact that the lives of these saints and blesseds throughout the history of the order have had on him. Thank you, Kevin, for sharing our family with the world in a fresh way as we celebrate this eight hundredth anniversary.

May the Hounds of the Lord increase and multiply, and may that torch continue to enlighten and enflame the world with knowledge of God's loving mercy, just as it has with Kevin Vost!

—Sister Matthew Marie, O.P.
Professor of Education
Aquinas College, Nashville

Barking Out the Word of God for Eight Hundred Years and Counting

---

Six hundred, six again, and yet sixteen,
These were the years since God's own human birth,
When, under Dominic, there first was seen
The Order that should preach to all the earth.[1]

The roving dogs are the Order of Preachers who do not wait at
their homes for the poor but go out to them and lick the ulcers
of their sins, having in their mouths the bark of preaching.
—Saint Albert the Great on Luke 16:19–21

In October of 2013 a coworker at my disability determination office told me that she, who is not a physician, faced the daunting task of teaching our latest policies on the adjudication of

---

[1] Cited in Simon Tugwell, *Early Dominicans: Selected Writings* (Mahwah, NJ: Paulist Press, 1982), 56. Tugwell notes that these doggerel verses found in A. Dondaine's *Jean de Mailly* are not original to de Mailly but are also found in the works of Robert of Auxerre of the Praemonstratensian Order.

heart disease cases to a room full of licensed cardiologists. It was especially easy to show her compassion, since I was faced with a similar task in the weeks ahead: one of giving a talk on All Saints' Day about none other, of all saints, but Dominic de Guzman—to a room full of habit-wearing, card-carrying Dominicans![2]

I explained to the faculty of Aquinas College of Nashville on that November 1 that, although I had written books influenced by Saint Thomas Aquinas, a Dominican of the first rank, and a biography of his great Dominican teacher, Saint Albert the Great, I was surely no expert on the life of Saint Dominic. In fact, I knew I had to do a great deal of what psychologists might euphemize as "undistributed learning," but which every student knows firsthand is really cramming—that frantic, feverish, bleary-eyed, coffee-driven, last-minute study before one takes a big test. And yet, as I told the professors in the audience, it soon occurred to me that I was not going to speak to them as an expert on Saint Dominic at all, but merely as a layperson who had been personally impacted for the good by the work of Saint Dominic and his holy Order of Preachers. In that sense, I had been preparing for that lecture for almost fifty years, since I started kindergarten at Saint Agnes School under the tutelage of the Dominican Sisters of Springfield, Illinois—and that made the task far less daunting.

A couple of Sundays before the talk, as I sat chatting in the backyard with my wife and our next-door neighbor, our neighbor said that earlier she had watched a televangelist whose whole focus was on Jesus Christ *as a traveling preacher*. She said it inspired her, and it was a message she was not used to hearing. I had to

---

[2]   Thanks again, Sister Matthew Marie, for that fateful invitation.

smile as I told her I was heading south in a couple of weeks to talk to a group of people whose whole lives are centered on just that notion—the imitation of Christ as a traveling preacher—and in fact, these Dominicans are officially known as the Order of Preachers.[3] I told her as well that in medieval Europe they were sometimes called (and called themselves) the "hounds of the Lord," a pun on their name, from the name of their founder, Saint Dominic, since the Latin word for "dog" or "hound" is *canis* and *Domini* means "of the Lord."[4]

I told our neighbor that the Dominicans' founder was particularly fond of Saint Matthew's Gospel, and that Gospel tells us that right after Jesus had collected his first disciples, "he went about all Galilee, teaching in their synagogues and preaching the gospel of the kingdom and healing every infirmity among the people" (Matt. 4:23). So there was Christ, nearly two thousand years ago in Galilee, *teaching, preaching,* and *healing.*

How interesting, I told my audience at Aquinas College in Nashville, operated by the Congregation of the Dominican Sisters of Saint Cecilia, that sitting in front of me was a room full of *preachers* and college *teachers.* Indeed, their two new graduate programs focused specifically on the training of teachers and *healers* (nurses), and right next door was Saint Thomas Hospital West. It seemed these Nashville Dominicans (like other Dominican groups throughout the world), had taken this *preaching, teaching,* and *healing* business pretty darn seriously!

---

[3]   Indeed, as one sister told me, perhaps tongue slightly in cheek: "Christ was the first Dominican!"

[4]   English speakers are familiar with furry, four-footed *canines* and with our notation for the years since the birth of Christ: A.D. (*Anno Domini*), "in the year of the Lord."

Anyway, for better or for worse, I was honored to give that talk on Saint Dominic and then to breathe a sigh of relief and get back to other business.

Well, we are supposed to learn from our mistakes (heaven forbid, especially when we're over fifty), and yet, almost a year to the day later, I found myself in an almost identical pickle. I was again scheduled to give a talk on a great Dominican saint, this time Saint Martin de Porres on his feast day, November 3, to faculty and students at another Dominican institution of higher learning (Mount Saint Mary's College in Newburgh, New York). I had certainly heard of and read a bit about Saint Martin, but I was once again in for a crash course of undistributed learning (i.e., cramming). Again, I was astounded and blessed by the opportunity to learn about such a wonderful Dominican saint and to share whatever fruits might have come from my contemplation of him. (I'll share some of those in Saint Martin's chapter in this book.)

So, a month or so went by, and I was back at home writing a book about the great Stoic philosophers and how their ideas based on human reason and natural law might be helpful for us Christians in training ourselves to control our emotions, build virtue, and strive to conform our wills to God's.[5] As I set aside my reading for the day, I happened to look at my bookmark. It had been given to me by the Nashville Dominicans the day I talked on Saint Dominic. It featured one of my favorite quotations from Saint Thomas's *Summa Theologica*: "For even as it is better to enlighten than merely to shine, so it is better to give to others

---

[5] *The Porch and the Cross: Ancient Stoic Wisdom for Modern Christian Living* (Kettering, OH: Angelico Press, 2015).

the fruits of one's contemplation than merely to contemplate."[6] It also mentioned an upcoming event: the Eight Hundredth Jubilee of the Order of Preachers in 2016. The Dominicans will soon have preached the gospel of Christ for a full eight hundred years — the "six hundred, six again, and then sixteen," of our opening quotation.

That bookmark was my "Aha!" We need a new popular book, I thought, to help celebrate the Jubilee of this wonderful order. The great Dominicans, I thought, were like "Stoics on spiritual steroids."[7] They have such great natural *and* supernatural treasures to offer. I thought we needed to present to modern lay readers the wonderful spiritual heritage and the ever-useful lessons of their great saints and blesseds. Thankfully, Charlie McKinney at Sophia Institute Press agreed.

Speaking of thanks, I would also like to acknowledge Michael Lichens and Nora Malone for their painstaking editing and formatting of this book. (If errors remain, please chalk them up to the overwhelming plethora they received from me.) I don't mind in the least if readers judge this book by its cover, and for that I thank Carolyn McKinney. Thanks are due as well to Sheila Perry and all the staff at Sophia Institute Press. Many thanks to Sister Matthew Marie Cummings, O.P., Ed.D., and all the good Dominican Sisters down in Nashville, for all their encouragement and inspiration. Thanks are due, as always, to my friend Shane Kapler, this time for pointing me to the writings of Venerable

---

[6] *Summa Theologica* (*ST*), II-II. Q. 188, art. 6.

[7] And those Stoics were no strangers to the Dominicans, I might add. Saint Albert the Great, Saint Thomas Aquinas, Blessed Humbert of Romans, and Blessed Raymond of Capua are among Dominicans who cite the Latin-writing Stoic Seneca in their writings.

Louis of Granada and to the very recent facial reconstruction work on Saint Rose of Lima that is mentioned in her chapter. Thanks to T. J. Burdick for his support of this effort (and of all efforts Thomistic and Dominican). Special thanks to my wife, Kathy, for tending our household so that I might sit, read, and write. Finally, thanks go out to you, my readers, and to God, through whom we all live and move and have our being.

Now, let's get down to business as I introduce you to some of the greatest Dominicans of the last eight hundred years, hounds of the Lord who have barked out Christ's gospel in the many-splendored ways they have showed us of how to think, do, and love for the glory of God and the salvation of countless souls.

Hounds of the Lord

Dominican Thinkers, Doers, and Lovers

In the communion of saints, many and varied spiritualities have been developed throughout the history of the churches. The personal charism of some witnesses to God's love for men has been handed on, like "the spirit" of Elijah to Elisha and John the Baptist, so that their followers may have a share in this spirit.
— Catechism of the Catholic Church, no. 2684

Those who are more adapted to the active life can prepare themselves for the contemplative by the practice of the active life; while, nonetheless, those who are more adapted to the contemplative life can take upon themselves the works of the active life, so as to become yet more apt for contemplation.
— Saint Thomas Aquinas,
Summa Theologica, II-II, Q. 182, art. 4

Throughout the history of the Church, there would seem to have been two distinct classes of saints. There are saints who personify active love and tenderness and there are saints who personify energetic action and the spirit of eager propagandism.
— Henri Joly, The Psychology of the Saints

"The Spirit" of Saint Dominic

The universe abounds in a mind-dazzling array of diverse things, from subatomic particles to galaxies, from stones, to plants, to animals, to man, all the way up to angels. Saint Thomas Aquinas wrote that God produced such an astounding number and variety of creatures because each and every thing that exists, in its own way, represents some small facet of God's divine goodness: "for goodness, which in God is simple and uniform, in creatures is manifold and divided; and hence the whole universe together participates in the divine goodness more perfectly, and represents it better than any single creature whatever."[8]

The one, holy, catholic, and apostolic Church reflects God in a somewhat similar way. The Catholic Church is *one*, as God is "simple and uniform," and indeed, Jesus Christ, who was one with the Father, prayed that His Church would be one.[9] The Communion of Saints, throughout time and in all lands, speaks to the Church's *catholicity* (universality) and points to the Creator of the universe itself. The "many and varied spiritualities" of those saints emanate from God as the source of all *holiness* and shows us the many ways in which we can strive to share in His holiness. The Church is *apostolic* too, in that she is founded on Christ's apostles, all of whom, in their own ways, participated in making known more perfectly to the ends of the earth the divine goodness of their Master and in passing down their mission throughout the ages in the apostolic succession of our popes and bishops.

How grand, as well, is the manifold goodness within the Church that is seen in the way in which the "many and varied

[8]   Saint Thomas Aquinas, *ST*, I, Q. 47, art. 1.
[9]   John 17:11–23.

spiritualities" of some great saints have given rise to vast, diverse, and enduring religious orders. Great monks, such as the Benedictines and the Cistercians, have helped us learn how to contemplate, how to work, and how to pray. The Franciscans have helped us appreciate the beauty and glories of God's creation, of our Brother Sun and Sister Moon, and have shown us what it can mean to imitate Christ in poverty and simplicity. Orders such as these and many others have been praying for our souls and healing our bodies for centuries. In my own city, many sick are cared for in a Franciscan hospital, and many students of all ages have been taught about God and the universe in schools of the Ursulines, the Viatorians, and the Benedictines.

Another holy order has been present as well, in my town and in many others. One group of its daughters provided my elementary education, and many decades later, I had the privilege to teach a bit for another group of its daughters at the graduate level, six hours south, in Nashville. Many readers have no doubt also benefited from the grace-filled labors of these special sons and daughters, the children who bear the spirit of their father Saint Dominic.

This, then, is the main concern of this book: to pass on from the perspective of a layman who owes so much to Dominicans a taste of that glorious and joyful spirit that they have for so long and so willingly shared. Even so, while they all share in one unifying Dominican spiritual brotherhood and sisterhood, it is manifested within that order in so many unique and beautiful ways. As modern authors relate an old saying, "If you've met one Dominican, you've met one Dominican."[10] One or more of these

---

[10] Robert Curtis, O.P.L., and Karen Woods, O.P.L., *Domincana: A Guidebook for Inquirers*, 2nd ed. (Raleigh, NC: Schoolboy Press, 2004), 206.

ways may speak to you, to inspire you to find new ways to spread the joy of Christ's gospel, to glorify God through your thoughts, words, and deeds, to let loose the "hound of the Lord" within you.

Legends, Lives, Lessons, and Legacies

The pages ahead hold the legends, lives, lessons, and legacies of nine great Dominican saints and blesseds.

Legends: Countless fascinating legends and pious stories have accrued in the hagiographies[11] of so many great Dominicans across the centuries and across the nations of the earth. Prophetic dreams and visions; apparitions of Christ, His Mother, and other great saints; appearances of the devil in disguise; miraculous healings galore; episodes of bilocation; stigmata; incorruption after death; and more. To call them legends does not imply that they are not true, for anything is possible with God, and the Scriptures themselves abound in such miracles. Rather, to call them legends implies that such events are grand and astounding—*legendary!* Indeed, we might ask ourselves, as we strive to become saints, what kind of legends we might wish our spiritual descendants would tell about us. Such legends as those we'll sample show how God favored these holy men and women in many surprising and supernatural ways, so keep your eyes and hearts open as vast tapestries of legendary miracles and deeds unfold.

Lives: Christ became incarnate, suffered death, was buried, and rose again for every single person. Every single person has his own story, and every life matters. Here we will draw from

---

[11] Written lives of the saints, from the Greek *hagio*, "holy" or "saintly," and *graph*, "writing."

available historical and biographical material to lay out in brief the highlights of the lives of Saint Dominic and eight of his most glorious sons and daughters. Choosing which lives to feature was no easy matter. Indeed, in the words of Pope Clement X from more than three hundred years ago:

> Do not ask me how many saints the Order of Saint Dominic has given to heaven. Count, if you can, the stars which gleam in the firmament, and then you will know the number of saints among the descendants of Saint Dominic.[12]

We will travel through several centuries and several nations as we highlight key events, key figures, and key ideas in the lives of each of these "stars" in God's heaven. With some, we will be blessed not only with writings about them but also with their own writings. With some, we will be able to examine their interactions with one another as they worked together within their holy order to bark out the good news of Christ. With all, we will be blessed with holy examples of the many effective ways Christ's gospel may be brought into the hearts of our next-door neighbors—and all the way to the ends of the earth.

Lessons: Now we arrive at the heart of each chapter, or, as Saint Thomas Aquinas might say, the "end." The end here refers not to the last pages, but to the primary purpose, goal, or reason for all of the pages of every saint's chapter. Our greatest concern in reading about these great saints and blesseds should be to mine the great lessons they teach us. Each imitated Christ in his own way and can inform and inspire us to imitate Him better in ways

---

[12] Cited in Dominican Novices, *Dominican Saints* (Rockford, IL: TAN Books, 1995), 410.

of our own. Some were great teachers and taught us explicitly in great works of philosophy, theology, or spiritual reflection. Others, like their founder and even Christ Himself, wrote hardly a word but taught invaluable lessons through the acts of their daily lives. To teach some people the important things of God, you just about have to draw them a picture. Well, one of the blessed Dominicans featured here did just that too and did so remarkably well (and in chapter 3 his story we will tell).

Legacies: Although they all passed from earth nearly a good century or more ago, every saint and blessed in these pages lives on with God in the afterlife. So as well as enriching us with their lessons and examples from their time on earth, they also stand ready to intercede for us in heaven. Keep on the lookout, then, for saints to whom you might turn for help and inspiration through their *heavenly* intercession. These great Dominicans have also provided us with great *earthly* legacies in a vast array of institutions such as hospitals, elementary schools, high schools, and universities. These institutions are full of living and breathing "hounds of the Lord" who continue to bless us as Christ did through ongoing teaching, preaching, and healing. So note well too that we will note well some of these present-day legacies.

Thinkers, Doers, and Lovers

We will employ some unique trifocal glasses as we examine these saints as "thinkers, doers, and lovers," as embodiments of the "contemplative, apostolic, and charitable spiritual styles." Two lenses for these glasses have themselves been prescribed by Dominicans, and indeed all three can be found in the four classic pillars of Dominican life.

Saint Thomas Aquinas notes that Pope Saint Gregory the Great had observed in his *Homily on Ezekiel:* "There is a twofold life wherein Almighty God instructs us by His holy word, the active and the contemplative."[13] Six hundred years later, over the course of twenty articles in four questions of the *Summa Theologica*,[14] Thomas considers in depth the meaning and significance of what Gregory has differentiated as the contemplative and the active lives. In a nutshell, the active life is to feed the poor, to instruct the ignorant, to love and to care for our neighbor in all his needs, as Christ instructed us. The contemplative life is to focus one's mind through prayer, study, and meditation on God Himself, desiring nothing but our Creator. They both correspond to the Great Commandments to love God with all that we are and to love our neighbor as ourselves.

The most striking biblical types of the two styles of spiritual life are depicted in Luke 10:38–42. When Jesus pays a visit to Martha's home, she scurries about, tending to the needs of the guests while her ostensibly lazy sister Mary simply sits at Christ's feet, listening to His teaching. Martha is active, and Mary is contemplative, and they both strive in their ways to serve the Lord and their neighbor.

Some of us are drawn more to one way of life than to the other, due to our inborn temperaments and dispositions. In modern parlance, some of us tend to be thinkers, and some of us tend to be doers. Which one are you? I place myself in the thinkers camp (at least, I think so). In the history of the religious life, various orders have focused more on either the contemplative or the active life. Consider, for example, the lives of monks, hermits,

---

[13] Saint Thomas Aquinas, *ST,* II-II, Qs. 179–182.
[14] Ibid., Q. 179, art. 1.

and cloistered nuns, whose primary focus is on contemplative prayer, as opposed to those of other orders who go out into the world building hospitals and schools, actively tending to the needs of their neighbors' bodies and souls.[15]

Of course, we don't want to set up too rigid a dichotomy here, for we are all called both to think and to act, as the Jesuits put it so well, *ad majorem Dei gloriam inque hominum salutem*, "for the greater glory of God and the salvation of man." Even the ancient monks of St. Benedict were known for their motto *ora et labora*—"pray and work." This great mission can be seen as well in the Dominicans—so famous for their proclivity toward study in the pursuit of truth that *Veritas*, "Truth," itself is their motto—who also hold true to a motto we came across earlier in the writings of Saint Thomas Aquinas: "For even as it is better to enlighten than merely to shine, so it is better to give to others the fruits of one's contemplation than merely to contemplate."[16]

With that said, we will still use this twofold division as two of our *three* special lenses in examining the lives of our saintly Dominicans. We'll identify the more active types in the first group, our doers of part 1, as having an "apostolic style," since what is the first priority within the Order of Preachers but to act as Christ's apostles, preaching His gospel to the ends of the earth? That is what holy doers do, and that's why we'll class them as "apostolic doers." The second group, the more contemplative types of part 2, those drawn especially to study, meditation, and prayer, are known for their great works of theology and for their

---

[15] Within the folds of the habits of the Dominican Order, there are groups of cloistered second-order contemplative nuns and of Third Order sisters who go out into the word in a variety of activite ministries, especially teaching and healing.

[16] Saint Thomas Aquinas, *ST*, II-II. Q. 188, art. 6.

zeal and focus in contemplating God. They are our "contemplative thinkers."

That's enough for starters on these two styles of spiritual life. Plenty of explication will come in the pages ahead. You will recall, however, that I spoke of *trifocal* glasses. So what is the *third* lens, and who prescribed it? Good questions! Well, we are going to split the active life into two: the "apostolic doers" and the "charitable lovers."

The nineteenth-century French Catholic psychologist Henri Joly once observed: "Throughout the history of the Church, there would seem to have been two distinct classes of saints. There are saints who personify active love and tenderness, and there are saints who personify energetic action and the spirit of eager propagandism."[17] Do you detect our "lovers" in addition to our "doers"? When Joly suggested these two classes, his first example of a saint who personified "active love and tenderness" was none other than Saint Dominic's holy friend Saint Francis of Assisi. And who held pride of place as the first example of a saint who embodied "energetic action and the spirit of eager propagandism"? None other than Saint Francis's holy friend Saint Dominic de Guzman!

This is not at all to say that Saint Dominic did not love fervently (we'll see how fervently he loved in our very next chapter) nor to say that Saint Francis was not a ball of energy and zeal! Still, it can be helpful to think of different "classes" of saints, so we can focus on what they are best known for and that it might bring out the best in us as well. For our purposes in this book, the distinction is partly a matter of scale. The apostolic doers will be those most known as great spiritual movers and shakers, founding

---

[17] Henri Joly, *The Psychology of the Saints* (Fort Collins, CO: Roman Catholic Books, n.d.), 50.

and growing great movements, becoming fishers of men, like the apostle Saint Paul—spurring countless souls to take on an entirely new way of life in preaching Christ's gospel in new ways and new places. The charitable lovers will be those best known for moving and shaking one soul at a time. These are the saints known for their tenderness, kindness, nurturing, and hospitality—those who, like Holy Mother Mary, do God's will and honor Christ by the nurturing love they provide for every person they meet.

So then, these three spiritual styles—the apostolic, the contemplative, and the charitable styles of the doers, the thinkers, and the lovers, if you will—will provide our special focus as we examine the legends, lives, lessons, and legacies of these nine great Dominicans.[18]

And don't worry in the least about any false "trichotomy," so to speak, for we will also examine every saint through *all three* of our lenses. They all knew that God has called us all to know Him, to love Him, and to do His will every day of our lives. As another great Dominican, Saint Richard of Chichester (1197–1253) put it:

> O most merciful Redeemer, friend and brother,
> May I know thee more clearly,

---

[18] Please don't doubt that it can be done! I've done it once before in *Three Irish Saints: A Guide to Finding Your Spiritual Style* (TAN Books, 2012). There, our apostolic doer was Saint Patrick, "Apostle to the Irish." Our contemplative was Saint Kevin of Glendalough, a hermit so intent on prayer and contemplation that he had to be discovered by a cow while praying in a hollow of a tree and carried out of his woods on a litter when God had some active work for him to do! Our charitable lover was Saint Brigid of Kildare, with a heart so full of love for all that some called her the "Other Mary."

love thee more dearly,
and follow thee more nearly, day by day.[19]

We should note as well the four famous and interlinked pillars of Dominican spirituality—prayer, study, preaching, and community. Dominican prayer and study are grounded in contemplation, preaching Christ's gospel is the fundamental call of their order, and the sons and daughters of Saint Dominic pray, study, preach, and live within the context of shared and loving communities. These pillars uphold their capacities to think, to love, and to do—or, as another of their mottos so boldly declares, *Laudare, benedicere, praedicare!* —"To praise, to bless, to preach!"

So Many Dominicans, So Few Pages; Ergo, More "Hounds of the Lord"

Speaking of Saint Richard of Chichester, and calling to mind so many other great Dominicans like him, we have added one more feature to this book to alleviate the pressure of reducing our focus to a mere nine saints and blesseds. This is where the "Hounds of the Lord" essays come in. At the end of each chapter we will provide a brief, one-page biography of additional hounds of the Lord, and not all of them saints or blesseds (yet). These will provide yet more opportunities for additional Dominicans, some closer to our time, to show us yet more ways to know God more clearly, love him more dearly, and follow him more nearly.

So, without further adieu, let's set loose the hounds of the Lord.

---

[19] Some will recognize these words in the song "Day by Day" made famous in the play and movie *Godspell* from the 1970s.

PART 1

Dominican Doers and the Apostolic Style

And how are they to hear without a preacher? And how can men preach unless they are sent? As it is written, "How beautiful are the feet of those who preach good news! . . . Their voice has gone out to all the earth, and their words to the ends of the world."
—Romans 10:14–15, 18

Saint Dominic de Guzman Lets Loose the Hounds of the Lord

The future greatness of her younger son was announced to Joanna even before his birth. The mysterious vision of a dog, bearing in his mouth a lighted torch which set fire to the world, appeared to indicate the power of that doctrine which should kindle and illuminate men's hearts through the ministry of his words.
—Sister Augusta Theodosia Drane,
The Life of Saint Dominic

It is doubtful if any other man, saint or not, accomplished so much in so short a lifetime, or expressed so unequivocally his faith in the future.
—Sister Mary Jean Dorcy, O.P., *Saint Dominic's Family*

A Dark World in Need of a Fiery Hero

Saint Dominic de Guzman was born in 1170 and died on August 6, 1221. The magnitude of his achievements was astounding for the half century that God allotted him on earth, but on his deathbed, he told his brother friars that he would do much more for them in the next life — and those words have rung true for nearly eight hundred years!

Dominic was born to his mother, Joanna (or Jane), and his father, Don Felix de Guzman, at their castle of Caleruega, in Old Castile, a mountainous region of north-central Spain. His lineage was a knightly one in the service of the kings of Spain and a holy one in the service of Christ the King. His uncle and two of his brothers were priests, and his mother and one brother would one day be beatified.[20]

Spain and the whole of Christendom were immersed in dark and trying times when the boy was born; his mother had received a vision in which she gave birth to a dog bearing a torch that would enlighten the world. Islamic Moors had long controlled part of Spain, and the Albigensian heresy was flourishing not far to the northeast in the Languedoc region of southern France. The Crusades raged on in the Holy Land, impacting all nations of Europe. By the time the boy had become a mature man, Pope Innocent III would call the Fourth Lateran Council that would last a full two and a half years (1213–1215), addressing not only vital theological issues such as transubstantiation and the primacy of the papacy, but a host of problems, including the continuing Muslim threat, the ongoing split with the Greek Church, the immoral behaviors of many in the clergy, and the need for good preaching and a better-educated clergy. Many of the pressing needs of the Church and of the world would be met by our foundational doer who let loose the hounds of the Lord and spread light that illuminates brightly even to our time.

---

[20] Blessed Jane of Aza, beatified in 1828 by Pope Leo XII, and Blessed Mannes de Guzman, beatified by Pope Gregory XVI in 1834.

First, we will take a quick look at the man in the words of a woman who knew him, Bl. Cecilia (1204–1290):

This was Saint Dominic's appearance. He was of middle height and slender figure, of handsome and somewhat ruddy countenance, his hair and beard auburn, and with lustrous eyes. From out his forehead and between his eyebrows a radiant light shown forth, which drew everyone to revere and love him. He was always joyful and cheerful, except when moved to compassion at anyone's sorrows. His hands were beautiful and tapering; his voice was clear, noble, and musical; he was never bald, but kept his religious tonsure entire, mingled here and there with a few grey hairs."[21]

Now, having looked this great saint in the lustrous eye, it is time to examine his life, legends, lessons, and legacies in light of the ways he thought, did, and loved.

"To Praise": Saint Dominic and the Contemplative Style

We will focus soon enough on Saint Dominic as the foundational and ultimate Dominican doer, but this great saint was a first-rate thinker as well. His heart burned with zeal to preach the good news, and he knew that to do so most effectively he needed to *know* that message by heart. Indeed, Brother John of Spain, the fifth sworn witness in his canonization process, would testify

---

[21] Blessed Cecilia Cesarine, *The Legend of Saint Dominic*, pt. 3, chap. 14, in Gerard de Frachet's *The Lives of the Brethren: The Early Years of the Order of Preachers*, trans. Placid Conway, O.P. (Lexington, KY: Imperium Christi Press, 2015), 107.

on August 10, 1233: "He always carried around with him the Gospel of Matthew and the letters of Paul, and he read them so often that he knew them by heart."[22] Saint Catherine of Siena, a spiritual daughter of the next century, would write: "Of a truth Dominic and Francis were two columns of the holy Church. Francis with the poverty which was specially his own, as has been said, and Dominic with his learning."[23]

Dominic knew well that to do what is good we must know what is *true*. We see this strong intellectual tradition carried on in the Dominican motto of *Veritas* (Truth), and as Dominic knew so well and felt so powerfully, the truth (as well as the way and the life) is Christ Himself. Dominic was a lover of books; he studied diligently to become a priest and a canon[24] attached to the cathedral at Osma, Spain. He recruited his novices especially from university settings and sent them to learn and to teach. In a few generations his spiritual sons would become the greatest of all professors in the world and theologians to the pope himself. Every Dominican convent would become a house of learning.

God has provided us with virtues to perfect our powers of thinking and contemplation. The three fundamental *intellectual virtues* of *science* (or knowledge — from *sciere*, "to know"), *understanding*, and *wisdom* may be found together in the Scriptures: "By wisdom a house is built, and by understanding it is established; by knowledge the rooms are filled with all precious and pleasant riches" (Prov. 24:3–4). These virtues were examined in depth

---

[22] Tugwell, *Early Dominicans*, 75.

[23] Saint Catherine of Siena, *Dialogues* 4.5, Christian Classics Ethereal Library, accessed August 17, 2015, http://www.ccel.org/ccel/catherine/dialog.iv.v.v.html.

[24] A member of a group of priests who lived in community and followed the Rule of Saint Augustine.

by pagan philosophers, including Aristotle in his *Nicomachean Ethics,* and raised to the heights of Christian understanding in the writings of a son of Saint Dominic, Saint Thomas Aquinas, in his *Commentary on Aristotle's Nicomachean Ethics* and within his own massive *Summa Theologica.*[25]

When Saint Catherine emphasized Dominic's special gift of learning, she used the Italian words *la scientia,* denoting that virtue of *science,* or knowledge. Saint Thomas would later explicate that the Holy Spirit's gift of understanding, which perfects the human virtue of understanding, is "a certain excellence of knowledge that penetrates into the heart of things"[26] and that it is aided foremost by a purity of heart, since Christ Himself stated: "Blessed are the pure in heart, for they shall see God" (Matt. 5:8). Saint Dominic maintained a purity of body and mind that enabled him to see God reflected in His creation on earth, before he would see him face-to-face in heaven. The highest of the intellectual virtues is *wisdom.* Aristotle once wrote that it is better to know a little about sublime things than a lot about mean or trivial things, and that sublime things are the subject matter of wisdom. Dominic never focused on the mean or the trivial but wisely kept his sights on God. Many of the brothers who testified at his canonization reported that Dominic rarely talked except *about* God and the things of God, or *to* God in prayer, and he encouraged his brothers to do the same. "Let us think about our Savior," he would frequently say, according to Brother Paul of Venice.[27]

---

[25] Saint Thomas Aquinas, *ST,* I-II, Qs. 57–58.

[26] Ibid., II-II, Q. 8, art. 3.

[27] Number eight of nine canonization witnesses, as cited in Tugwell, *Early Dominicans,* 82.

Dominic continually worked to build those intellectual virtues, the oars with which he rowed toward truth, but even more importantly, he was always receptive to the Holy Spirit's corresponding gifts of knowledge, understanding, and wisdom,[28] powerful winds God put behind his sails.[29] Saints Albert the Great and Thomas Aquinas, two of the greatest thinkers of all time, were particularly known for the ways in which they used their intellectual virtues and gifts to *integrate* or *synthesize* — to reconcile, put together, and make sense of abstract and difficult subject matter, and oftentimes of conflicting opinions and approaches to knowledge. We'll get to all that in part 2, but for now I will note that these saints inherited this trait from their spiritual father, for Saint Dominic was also a great synthesizer of some very profound truths. Some have noted that Dominic did not create novelties so much as he joined and brought together in new ways great traditions and lessons from the past. Here I will briefly highlight just a few of his greatest syntheses:

- *Matter* and *spirit*: Dominic fought Albigensianism, a heresy in Southern France that sprang from Manichaean roots that considered the material realm and the body as evil and only the realm of the spirit as good. Dominic was a champion of the goodness of all of creation and of the reality of Christ in His Incarnation. One of the earliest stories of his preaching successes was when he stayed up all night

---

[28] Along with *counsel, piety, fortitude,* and *fear of the Lord* (cf. Isa. 11:2–3).

[29] Saint Thomas would later explain that whereas natural virtues allow our thoughts and actions to be guided by human reason, the gifts of the Holy Spirit bring them under the Spirit's guidance (see Saint Thomas Aquinas, *ST*, I-II, Q. 68).

in conversation and won an Albigensian innkeeper back to the fullness of truth of the Church.

- *Body* and *soul*: Dominic did not see us as souls trapped in bodies but as ensouled bodies, as mind-soul unities whose bodies and souls both are gifts from God. He knew by heart the words of Saint Paul: "Glorify God in your body" (1 Cor. 6:20), and he sought to praise God through his body. Those who knew him have detailed nine ways in which Dominic prayed using different bodily postures, including bowing, lying down, standing, stretching, reading, walking, and more. Even today, these nine ways can lead all of us to a greater harmony of body and soul for the greater glory of God.[30]

- *Apostolic simplicity* and the *complex institutions of the medieval Catholic Church*: Many people in the twelfth and thirteenth centuries believed that the Church in many ways had moved away from and contrary to the spirit of the gospel as it was lived in the time of Christ and His apostles. This paved the way for heretical movements that claimed to have reclaimed that old-time religion of apostolic simplicity by discarding the Catholic Church. Dominic understood there was need for reform, but he knew as well the indispensability and indestructibility of the Church that Christ had built on the rock that

---

[30] The nine ways are presented in Tugwell's *Early Dominicans*. For an online source with photo illustrations see the Sisters of Saint Cecilia's website, http://nashvilledominican.org/ Charism/St_Dominic/Nine_Ways_of_Prayer.

was Peter. (We'll examine how he did this when we look at him as a doer.)

- *The contemplative* and the *active life*: The order Saint Dominic founded created a synthesis between the contemplative and active lives, the life of prayer and study and the life of active evangelization, the life of secluded stability and the life of itinerant preachers, life in the country and life in the city. Dominic and his brethren would pray and study in order to preach the good news. Indeed, he would shorten certain prayers and lighten certain duties so that his Friars Preachers would not be unnecessarily hindered in their first and foremost calling to preach the news of Christ and to bring Christ's salvation to the souls of their neighbors, even to the ends of the earth.

"To Preach": Saint Dominic and the Apostolic Style

"Be doers of the word, and not hearers only" (James 1:22). This was a message Saint Dominic took to heart all his life, and what did this consummate doer strive the most to do? In Christ's words, to "go into all the world and preach the gospel to the whole creation" (Mark 16:15). This was Saint Dominic's burning objective, the salvation of souls, and his contemplative acts of prayerful study and teaching were the means to accomplish this apostolic end. This is where Dominic displayed that "energetic action and eager zeal to spread the faith" like few before him or since. To Saint Dominic, to be a doer was to become an apostle for Christ and to produce more disciples as zealous as he was.

Another masterful doer and tireless preacher, in many ways like Saint Dominic, Saint Patrick, the "Apostle to the Irish," once wrote in his *Confessio*, "I preached and still preach to strengthen and confirm your faith. I wish you would all strive to do bigger and better things. This would be my glory for the wise son is his father's glory." Patrick gave birth to an entire island nation of saints, of holy sons and daughters who redounded upon his and God's glory. Eight hundred years later and five hundred or so miles to the southeast, Dominic gave birth to a continent of his own saints, who soon spread around the world doing bigger and better things.

Doers engaged in the apostolic life must possess the moral cardinal virtues. These are the virtues that allow us to achieve the good, and Dominic possessed them to a heroic degree.[31] His self-control, born of *temperance*, was remarkable — he wore the simplest of habits, had no room of his own, ate sparsely, remained chaste and sober throughout his life — yet he did not err on the side of deficiency in this virtue by failing to recognize that things of the body are inherently good in their proper measure. He was a temperate man, but certainly not a joyless one.

Blessed Cecilia relates a captivating story: one evening Dominic paid a visit to a convent, and he asked the cellarer to bring up a large cup of wine. After drinking some himself, he invited all the brethren to do the same. And then he called out, "'I want all my daughters to have a drink.' ... Then all the sisters drank from it ... and they all drank up as much as they wanted, encouraged by Saint Dominic, who kept on saying, 'Drink up,

---

[31] In the words of canonization witness Brother Frugerio of Pennabilli, "He was adorned with all the virtues in such a degree that I never saw anyone like him." Cited in Tugwell, *Early Dominicans*, 85.

my daughters!' At that time there were 104 sisters there, and they all drank as much wine as they wanted."[32] Dominic knew well that Christ's first miracle changed water into wine, and he wanted his sons and daughters "drunk," in a metaphorical sense, on the wine that is Christ's joyous gospel message.

Dominic's *fortitude* was also truly remarkable. Fortitude is the virtue that endures the difficult to achieve the good, and Dominic gladly faced any obstacles to bring to others the good of salvation. He traveled great distances on foot throughout Europe, often in bare feet over unyielding ground, preaching to all who would hear him along the way. If he would trip on a stone along the way, he'd call out in delight that he was doing penance, and he would not put his shoes back on until he arrived at his destination. He was so enduring in his prayer and preaching that he sometimes fell asleep at prayer late at night, even at dinner and even before the altar. He frequently expressed the willingness to be martyred for Christ as well, if that should be God's plan for him.

Dominic also embodied the practical wisdom of *prudence* as he crafted the means to reach his holy goals. His Order of Preachers was established by papal bull on December 22, 1216, and by the end of his life, just five years later, he and his order were already fanning out in great numbers, preaching the gospel toward the end of the earth in their five established provinces, with six more in the works.

To encapsulate Dominic's work as a doer in one word, that word would certainly be ... *preacher,* and moving to our last

---

[32] Blessed Cecilia, *Miracula*, 6, cited in Paul Murray, O.P., *The New Wine of Dominican Spirituality: A Drink Called Happiness* (New York: Burns and Oates, 2008), 47.

cardinal virtue, here we see Saint Dominic's love for *justice* embodied in his zeal for preaching. Justice renders to each person his rightful due. Dominic believed all men and women had a right to learn the pathway to their salvation, and he had an obligation to make darn sure that they knew it! His grace of preaching was so powerful and his zeal to preach so intense that witnesses report that he often wept while he preached and made his listeners do the same.

"To Bless": Saint Dominic and the Charitable Style

Although Joly classified him as doer, and I am following suit, there was no doubt in the mind of anyone who knew him that Saint Dominic was also the most fervent of *lovers*. Saint Thomas, among others, has compared love to a furnace, and the more powerful the furnace, the further will its heat extend. Dominic strove to bring that white-hot love to the very ends of the earth. He sought to bring Christ to the pagan Cumans of modern-day Hungary and to the Muslim Saracens. The furnace of his love reached so far that it is said he wept even for the damned.

Joly had compared and contrasted the lives of worldly "great men" with the lives of the saints. He repeated an old saying that "no great man is a hero to his valet." In other words, sometimes those whose ambitions spread far and wide are not so good to those who are right under their noses. Thomas had noted, however, that as a powerful furnace carries its heat afar, those closest to it should get the most heat, and so too with the loving fires of charity. Charity, after all, begins at home, and those who knew Saint Dominic best also loved him the most. "He was happy, kind, patient, cheerful, compassionate, a comforter of the brethren," said Brother Rudolph of Faenza, a priest in charge of Saint Nicholas of the Vines in Bologna. Indeed, he reported, "I never saw a man whose service of God pleased me more than did that of the blessed Dominic."[33]

Thomas called charity a friendship with God, and we see friendship cherished and displayed in the actions of Saint Dominic. Consider how he sent his preachers out in twos, so that they might support and buttress each other. Ancient Greek thinkers described true friendship as "two hearts within one breast." A loving Christian is empathetic to the needs of his friend, attentive to ways he might reach out to serve him in a proactive way. Christ told us, after all, to *do* unto others as we would have them do unto us, not just to *react* to them.

Psychotherapist Alfred Adler used to say in reference to therapy clients that empathetic therapists "see with their eyes and hear with their ears." Well, Dominic was the most empathetic friend and comforter, seeing with his friends' eyes, hearing with their ears, and feeling with their hearts. In a true story both amazing and amusing, one Brother Stephen of Spain reported that one evening after he had confessed his sins to Dominic, he was eating dinner with some friends when two men came to tell him that Dominic said he was to come and see him. He told them to go away and that he'd come after dinner. They told him that Dominic said he was supposed to come *now!* He got up from the table and went with the two men, only to find the church of Saint Nicholas full of many Dominicans. Dominic told them to show Stephen how to do a *venia*[34] because Dominic had decided

---

[33] Cited in Tugwell, *Early Dominicans*, 77.
[34] A ritual prostration.

to admit him that night to the order. Dominic clothed him in the habit, saying: "I am giving you arms with which you will be able to fight the devil all the days of your life."[35]

Oddly enough, Stephen did not recall that he had ever spoken with Dominic about joining the order! It was not that Stephen was complaining, though, since he said he thought Dominic must have received some kind of divine revelation or inspiration about the matter. Stephen's testimony was made fifteen years after the event as the seventh witness in Dominic's canonization process, and Stephen had become, by the time of his testimony, the Dominican provincial in charge of Lombardy.

There are also many stories of Saint Dominic's caring tenderness in the simple, small things in life, as when Blessed Sister Cecilia reported that when he came home to Bologna from Spain, he brought for each of the Sisters a wooden spoon that the Sisters would forever cherish.

There was also a very special way that Saint Dominic was a lover, and that was in his role as a *father* of an order and of a family of saints. We are told to honor our fathers and our mothers, and we honor Dominic as a great spiritual father. Indeed, his very order would thrive partly because of the way it honored the great Church Fathers. It was said of Saint Thomas Aquinas, for example, that he so honored the Fathers of the Church, that he, in a way, inherited the intellect of them all.

Dominic's love for his brothers can be seen in his humble desire to be buried under their feet, as he was in Bologna, at the age of fifty-one, after a period of illness. In a way, all Dominicans are his children and the fruits of his contemplation.

---

[35] Tugwell, *Early Dominicans*, 79.

Dominic wrote little, and we don't have much more than one of his brief letters to Sisters in Madrid. In it he told them he was delighted with their way of life and thanked God for them. He exhorted them, saying, "May you make progress every day!" Countless Dominicans have progressed in countless ways in the third of a million days since he wrote those words.

Let's move along then to see just what kind of progress some of his sons and daughters have made.

Blessed Jordan of Saxony

1190–1237 | FEAST: FEBRUARY 13

Some biographers have styled Blessed Jordan as a holy thief of sorts, since he stole so many sons from their homes and so many students and professors from their universities by convincing them to join the new order and become hounds of the Lord! It was not until around the age of thirty that this German of noble lineage, then a student at the University of Paris, would don the habit of the Dominicans. The next year found him the provincial of Lombardy, and the year after that, the successor of Saint Dominic himself as master general of the entire order.

The new master general proved himself to be a master recruiter as well. His intelligence, eloquence, humor, joy, and kindly demeanor drew more than a thousand new novices as the order spread under his care from eight provinces to a full dozen. Among the recruits Blessed Jordan drew in are the subjects of chapters 2 and 4—Blessed Humbert of Romans and Saint Albert the Great. A doer extraordinaire, but a well-rounded thinker and lover as well, Blessed Jordan added an academic chair for the order at the University of Paris, helped found the University of Toulouse, and fostered learning within the Dominican Order, and he had such a great love for Saint Dominic that he would write a biography (still extant) among his several works.

Some of Blessed Jordan's most interesting surviving writings consist of fifty letters he wrote to Blessed Diana d'Andalo and the community of Dominican women with her at the convent in Bologna. These letters of friendship, spiritual direction, and consolation are a still a joy to read, as they so aptly demonstrate how a man and a woman can be loving friends in Christ.[36]

[36] See Gerald Vann, O.P., *To Heaven with Diana! A Study of Jordan of Saxony and Diana d'Andalo with a Translation of the Letters of Jordan* (iUniverse, 2006).

Blessed Humbert of Romans
Puts the Order in Order

It belongs to the wise man to order.
—Saint Thomas Aquinas, *Summa Contra Gentiles*

The contribution of Humbert of the Romans to
Dominican life can never be overestimated.
—Sister Mary Jean Dorcy, O.P., *Saint Dominic's Family*

They are also called dogs. "Dumb dogs which cannot bark"
(Is. 56:10). This is glossed, "Bark, that is, preach." So
the preacher is called a dog, and therefore ought to wander
round hither and thither like a hungry dog, eager to swallow
up souls into the body of the church. "They will feel
hunger like dogs and go about the city" (Ps. 58:7).
—Blessed Humbert of Romans,
On the Formation of Preachers 2.6.155

Deemed Blessed by His Soldiers of Christ

After Dominic's death on August 6, 1221, Blessed Jordan of
Saxony became the order's second master general. Raymond of

Penafort followed Jordan, Johannes von Wildeshausen followed Raymond, and Blessed Humbert of Romans, the great doer of this chapter, became the fourth successor to Saint Dominic as the fifth master general of the Order of Friars Preachers in 1254.[37]

Humbert has not been officially beatified as a blessed, but the Dominicans have been, in fact, so blessed by his actions, that he has long been called Blessed Humbert within the order. He was born at Romans, in Dauphine, to the southeast of France "around the year 1200"[38] and died on July 14, 1277. He went to Paris to obtain a master of arts and also studied canon law. There is an interesting legend of how he came to the order in 1224. He had been oscillating in his choice of vocation. He had considered becoming a Carthusian monk, and his brother had already done so. One day, at the Cathedral of Notre Dame, while chanting the Office of the Dead with the canons, an old priest struck up a conversation and asked him if he recalled his baptismal vows to renounce the devil and all his pomps, and asked then why shouldn't he become a Friar Preacher?[39] As

[37] Although the title master general may sound quite majestic to our ears, Saint Dominic had rejected the traditional title of abbot (father) for the leader of his democratic order, believing *magister* (meaning teacher rather than ruler) was a more humble and fitting title. Dominic himself and Dominican priests, as well as lay brothers, to this day call themselves "brothers."

[38] Per Tugwell, *Early Dominicans*, 32; Sister Dorcy reports the year of his birth as 1193. Sister Mary Jean Dorcy, O.P., *Saint Dominic's Family* (Rockford, IL: TAN Books, 1983), 83. With rather high infant mortality and a paucity of official records, the date of a medieval person's death is usually known with much greater accuracy than the year of his birth.

[39] It merits recalling Dominic's words to Stephen of Spain when he suddenly inducted him into the order: "I am giving you arms

Humbert pondered those words, and at the responsory "Where shall I fly if not to You?" (cf. Ps. 139:7), he decided to join the Order of Friars Preachers and flew, so to speak, to Blessed Jordan of Saxony, then master general, who bestowed on him the Dominican habit.

With his deep love for and knowledge of the Scriptures, Humbert was made a lecturer in theology at Lyon. Around 1238 he was elected provincial of the Roman Province, and here his *chrisma gubernationis*, or God-given talent for administration, a true mark of a doer, rang out so clear that by 1241 he received many votes in the papal election. By 1244 or 1245, he was elected provincial of France and in 1254, master general of the entire order, a post that he held for nine years.

Humbert's vast catalog of works as a provincial and master general included producing a standard Dominican lectionary, standardizing the Dominican liturgy, defending the Dominican chairs at the University of Paris against attacks by secular professors, mending fences with fellow mendicant Franciscans by issuing a joint encyclical with the their minister general, collecting hagiographical material on the lives of the then two Dominican saints (Dominic and Peter Martyr), providing a united constitution for Dominican nuns and a new edition of the constitutions for the brothers, negotiating agreements involving problems with the constitutions of the Carthusians, helping King Louis IX of France settle a dispute among three noble houses, and writing a commentary on the Rule of Saint Augustine that Saint Dominic had chosen to guide the Dominicans.

---

with which you will be able to fight the devil all the days of your life."

Despite all these accomplishments and more, this chapter will zoom in on and pursue doggedly just one of his works, one that defines him as a doer and defines what the hounds of the Lord do best: bringing healing and salvation through the barking of their preaching. Simon Tugwell, O.P., notes that Humbert's great work, *On the Formation of Preachers*, was apparently not well and widely received in Humbert's time, considering that although several copies of its various overlapping parts (including, for example, an extensive appendix of sample sermons) exist, not a single copy of the entire manuscript has been found. Thanks to Father Tugwell, though, the heart of Humbert's book is easily accessible now for any English speaker, preserved in his *Early Dominicans*. Humbert displays a fiery passion for preaching, an amazing grasp of its essential elements and of all of the relevant nuances, and a masterful penchant for all sorts of scriptural metaphors.

We will focus, then, on Humbert's *lessons*, summarizing the seven books or parts of Humbert's treatise on preaching, examining from almost every imaginable angle how Humbert and all Dominicans, in the role of preacher, have no choice but to be thinkers, doers, and lovers.

Prologue: Consider Thy Ministry

Blessed Humbert begins *On the Formation of Preachers* with a scriptural citation: "See that you fulfil the ministry which you have received in the Lord" (Col. 4:17). He explains that we cannot do a job well if we do not know well what it involves, noting that Saint Paul provided this advice to the archbishop who undertook preaching to the Colossians because he knew the lesson of 1 Samuel: 2–3: the sons of Eli were worthless as priests because they did not know what the job entailed.[40] This, then, is the goal Humbert lays out for his work: that preachers should be enabled with careful reflection to understand the job God has laid before them so that they might fulfill their ministry in the way God intended.

Humbert lays out his plan under seven general topics (to shorten and paraphrase):

- the job description
- what a preacher needs
- right and wrong ways of preaching
- the actual performance of preaching
- how people come to lack preaching
- the fruits of preaching
- things that go along with the job

The master general, then, generally masters the whole of the grace and art of preaching, enlightening the preacher's mind and prompting salivation for salvation in the hounds of the Lord in ways that even Pavlov just would not understand.

Preacher: Job Description

In defining the characteristics of the job of the preacher, Humbert provides six sections examining the job's nobility, how the

---

[40] After the prologue, Tugwell includes 563 numbered paragraphs from *On the Formation of Preachers*, and the vast majority of them are built on or include a specific scriptural quotation, some more than one. Some modern Christians call the Catholic Church "unbiblical." Perhaps they should read Blessed Humbert of Romans!

world needs it, how it is acceptable in God's eyes, how it profits the preacher himself, how it helps others, and how hard it is to do well.

Preaching's nobility is unquestionable, since it was the job Christ assigned to His apostles: "He appointed twelve, to be with him, and to be sent out to preach" (Mark 3:14). Next, citing scriptural texts for each argument, Humbert declares that preaching is not only apostolic but is also angelic, divine, and noble because it is based on Scripture, which surpasses the minds of men, deriving from the mind of God; because it is concerned not merely with things of the mind or of nature but with the things of God; because it serves the needs not merely of temporal life but of eternal life; because it serves the needs not merely of the body but of the soul; and as a service performed for a king is more important than a service performed for horses (!), so too do we see the exalted status of the job of the preacher who serves the King in ministering to the highest part of his highest creature.

Next, with a host of citations from Scripture and a few from Pope Saint Gregory the Great, Humbert provides twenty-two literal and metaphorical arguments showing how necessary preaching is in the ways it enlarges the kingdom of God, draws souls away from hell, makes the world fruitful, casts out demons, opens people's hearts to the hope of heaven, opens heaven to barbarian peoples, establishes the Church and guides her progress, brings forth light from darkness, checks all sorts of sins and wickedness, provides medicine to spiritual wounds, leads to wise government, and acts like life-giving rain to lands of spiritual drought.

Preaching is acceptable to the eyes of God in many striking ways. Here Humbert provides allegorical interpretations of

scriptural passages and their glosses[41] comparing preaching to
singers (Neh. 7:73; Song of Sol. 2:14), to hunters (Jer. 16:16;
Gen. 25:28; 27:3, 7), to those zealous for souls who provide a
sweet sacrifice (2 Cor. 11:2; Gen. 8:21), to soldiers of Christ (2
Tim. 2:3; 2 Macc. 12:11, 19; Zech. 9:8; 1 Sam. 29:6), to those
who bring souls to God (Wisd. 11:27), to God's envoys who han-
dle His missions (Eph. 6:20; 2 Cor. 5:20; Prov. 25:13), to God's
workmen (3 Kings 5:6; Prov. 8:31), to peddlers doing spiritual
business (Job 28:8; 1 Cor. 9:19; Luke 19:13; Matt. 25:21), and
to God's servants (Psalm 63:10; Prov. 14:35). Indeed, citing the
Song of Solomon 8:13, not only God, but his "friends" want to
hear the preachers, those friends being "the angels and the spirits
of the just who are with God."[42]

Those in the Order of Preachers surely seek the salvation
of their own souls as well as the souls of those to whom they
preach, and Humbert lays out a variety of intriguing reasons why
preaching can be of such help to the preacher himself in the
present life and in the hereafter. As for the bodily needs of this
life, the Lord said that those who preach the gospel are to live by
it as well (cf. 1 Cor. 9:14). Christ told His preachers to have no
anxiety or care for tomorrow (Matt. 6:26–32), to carry no bag or
wallet (Luke 10:4) and yet they would lack nothing (Luke 22:35).
As for the spiritual boons of preaching: "He who makes others
drunk will himself be made drunk too" (cf. Prov. 11:25). The
Gloss on this says: "The one who makes his hearers drunk with
the words of God will himself be made drunk with a draught of

---

[41] Humbert does this in every section. Here I will give but a taste
to whet your appetite for Humbert's complete treatise.

[42] Is that not a captivating image, the angels and saints with God
in heaven rejoicing in the preaching of preachers on earth?

manifold blessing."[43] This metaphorical drunkenness means the gift of an increase in interior grace. God also graces preachers with eloquence, with knowledge of what to say, with power to proclaim the word and generate devotion in some hearers so that they will shower prayers upon the preacher. And God gives the preacher spiritual children. As Saint Paul put it to his spiritual children in Corinth: "I became your father in Christ Jesus through the gospel" (1 Cor. 4:15). In sum, in this life, those who preach will be given the necessities of life, many spiritual gifts, and the devotion of their hearers. As for the next life: "[T]hose who turn many to righteousness, [shall shine] like the stars for ever and ever" (Dan. 12:3) and "shall be called great in the kingdom of heaven" (Matt. 5:19).

As to the aid that preaching gives to the preacher's spiritual progeny, Humbert mines the Scriptures to show how preaching the gospel enlivens the spirits of people who live in their bodies like corpses in tombs, how it gives people spiritual food to live on, nourishing indeed, and "sweet" words too (Ps. 119:103), how it raises to the spiritual realm those who live according to the senses alone, how it heals sick souls, breaks hardened hearts, and acts "like a powerful soap" that lifts the filth of sin and makes unlikely souls into saints.

The job of the preacher is no easy thing. Humbert tells us there are only a few *good* preachers, but in the primitive Church there were few preachers *at all*, yet they were so good that they converted the world! Preaching is a difficult art because many learned men try to preach without much in the way of results. This difficulty is seen in the way the art of preaching is learned. Aristotle famously said we become builders by builders and

[43] Tugwell, *Early Dominicans*, 195.

harpists by playing the harp,[44] and yet a man cannot make himself a successful preacher solely through his own efforts. "But a grace of preaching is had only by God's special gift. So it says, 'The ability of a man is in the hand of God' (Ecclus. [Sir.] 10:5).' 'Man' means 'preacher,' according to the Gloss." There is only one true teacher of this art as well: the Holy Spirit. As we see in Acts 2, the preaching of Peter and the apostles begins only *after* the Holy Spirit descended on them on Pentecost.

How does the preacher cooperate with the Holy Spirit to surmount the difficulty of his task? Three things are particularly helpful: *study, observation,* and *prayer.*

Although God provides a grace of preaching, the preacher must still *study* to make sure his preaching is commendable. Indeed, even the angels who held the seven trumpets *prepared themselves* to play their instruments (Rev. 8:6). Here we see Humbert the thinker, reminding preachers of Saint Jerome's comments on Ezekiel 3:1, "Eat the book": "The words of God should be stored up in our hearts and carefully examined, and only then proffered to the people."[45] Good preachers will eat and digest the good books of Scripture, not because they seek renown for the wit of their tongues but to study what is useful. Preachers will keep their sermons of reasonable length as well, so they don't give their hearers indigestion! Some preach with nothing but *rational arguments*, others with nothing but *anecdotes*, and yet others by *citing authorities*. The good preacher does *all three* in the right proportions. Indeed, when all three work together,

---

[44] A pithy modern parallel is "Practice makes perfect." For Humbert, as for preaching, only *God* makes perfect.

[45] Tugwell, *Early Dominicans*, 205.

the "hook of preaching" hangs from a strong triple line, "a line which no fish can easily break."[46]

As for *observation*, the good preacher observes good preachers and not-so-good ones as well, so that he can see what works well and what doesn't. Gideon is a symbol of a good preacher, and he says, "Look at me, and do likewise" (Judg. 7:17).

Last, but never least, is *prayer*. Man can achieve nothing purely on his own, but everything with God. Prayer is therefore, for the preacher, the most important thing of all. The preacher should petition God for help in overcoming the difficulties of this immensely difficult, but eminently worthy calling.

What a Preacher Needs

A preacher needs a holy conscience that comes from living a godly life, one beyond reproach, marked by austerity and penance, but also with a certain radiance so that his life might shine like a light among men through the harmony and integrity of his words and his deeds. Such a reputation will spread like perfume, likening the preacher to the apostles, who are the "aroma of Christ" (2 Cor. 2:15).

Every preacher is a thinker in that he needs many kinds of knowledge, including knowledge of Holy Scripture, of God's creatures (indeed, "this is why Saint Anthony said that creation is a book"), of important, edifying historical stories of both believers and of unbelievers, of the Church's precepts and her mysteries, of personal experiences, of the kind of discretion to know when to preach and when not to, and finally, knowledge of the Holy Spirit, for it was the Holy Spirit who taught the apostles to preach (Act 2:4).

[46] Tugwell, *Early Dominicans*, 206.

A preacher must also have an ability to speak, a good facility with words, buttressed by a good memory, a sonorous voice — indeed, Scripture often compares the voice of a preacher to a trumpet's blast: "Let there be a trumpet in thy throat" (Hos. 8:1, Douay-Rheims) — a balanced and moderate enunciation, speaking neither so quickly that it leads to confusion nor so slowly that it leads to boredom,[47] an ability to speak concisely[48] and simply, to speak in different ways suitable for different audiences, and last, but not least, "all of these will be of little value unless there is a graciousness upon the lips," for "a man without grace is like an idle tale" (cf. Ecclus. 20:21, Douay-Rheims), and as was said of the greatest of preachers, "grace is poured upon your lips" (Ps. 45:2).

The preacher also needs spiritual merit and will lose it if he departs from the truth in his preaching, does not practice what he preaches to others, seeks glory for himself rather than for God, preaches out of envy rather than goodwill (cf. Phil. 1:15), upsets people by harsh language, or inveighs so much against one fault that it engenders another (for example, humility must not be preached in such a way that it makes the timid more fearful and the proud more arrogant), preaches without any signs of penance, or preaches without charity (becoming like a tinkling cymbal: 1 Cor. 13:1).

[47] Here Humbert provides an example of knowledge useful to preachers that can come from unbelievers, citing the Stoic philosopher, statesman, and orator Seneca: "The philosopher's enunciation, like his life, ought to be orderly." (Indeed, Humbert cites Seneca approvingly five times within his treatise on preaching.)

[48] Here Humbert cites the Roman poet Horace: "Whatever you command, be brief, that what you say men's learning minds may quickly grasp and store away."

The preacher of Christ's gospel is to be a male, according to Scripture (1 Tim. 2:12) and is to be whole and strong in body to avoid public ridicule and to be able to endure staying up late at night studying, preaching loudly, extensive traveling, and poverty. He must be of the proper age, for even Christ waited to preach until He was thirty years old, having "reached the fullness of maturity in years" (cf. Eph. 4:13). He must also attain some kind of superiority over his listeners in terms of education or religious life, although at times preaching to one's superiors can be a positive exercise. Lastly, his life should not be in any way contemptible. As Gregory says, "If a man's life is despised, it will follow that his preaching too is despised."

Humbert concludes his section on a preacher's needs with a fascinating catalog of scriptural figures that symbolize preachers. He then provides about twenty-five of them, along with the scriptural references, which I'll provide in a chart at the end of this chapter. Humbert also summarizes the symbols according to nine categories: God, angels, the Church, heaven, the sky, the earth, things that fly, things that go bump in the night,[49] earthbound creatures, and human responsibilities.

Right and Wrong Ways of Preaching

Humbert asserts that there are three wrong ways to become a preacher: (1) becoming a preacher when something is lacking in a man, (2) becoming a preacher due to improper desire, and (3) taking the job in an arrogant or improper way.

As for something lacking, a man should not become a preacher who has not been purged of faults. Isaiah said, "Here

---

[49] I added that one myself. Just making sure you're still paying attention.

am I! Send me" (6:8), but only after he had been purged by the coal from the fire. Even those who have been purged should not preach before they've received the fullness of the Holy Spirit: "They were filled with the Holy Spirit and began to speak" (Acts 2:4). As Saint Bernard advised, the preacher should be a bowl, not a pipe. A pipe receives and pours out all at once, but the bowl waits until it's full and then overflows. The preacher should be overflowing in charity, strong in virtues, and dead to pride.

As for improper desire, preaching should not be motivated by ambition or desire for vainglory because of the honor that comes to teachers and preachers. As James (3:1) advised, "Let not many of you become teachers, my brethren." Those who teach and preach will be more harshly judged if they pervert their calling and use it to serve their own worldly desires. Neither should preachers be motivated to excel other preachers in fame.

As for an arrogant attitude, men are not fit for preaching who are eager to preach when they have little knowledge, who scheme to obtain a preacher's job, or who are insulted if they are not chosen as preachers.

If a man should take on the job of a preacher before the proper time, he will not produce fruits in others, will stunt his own development, and may fall into disaster like birds who try to fly before their wings are borne and fall to the earth from the heights. No, the teacher must wait until he is clothed with divine power, for God commanded His preachers, "Stay in the city, until you are clothed with power from on high" (Luke 24:49).

The Performance of Preaching

It can be a grave fault for a person not to preach when God has prepared him and listeners are ready. In the eloquent words of

Saint Bernard, "You are retaining possession of your neighbor's property if you tie up in a useless, indeed, a damnable silence, the word which you have the gifts of knowledge and eloquence to speak, and which would have brought benefit to many if you had spoken it."[50]

Sometimes people are dissuaded from preaching by trivial reasons such as an inappropriate lack of confidence and a sense of inadequacy, the assumption of false humility, or indeed, because they so love the tranquillity of contemplation that they seek to avoid the call to the active duties of preaching.[51] Some hold back because they are afraid they will be tempted to sin in the travels and dealings with others. Humbert asks, however, if it isn't better for a man to work and to pick up a little dust rather than stay clean while sitting at home? Others are held back because they continually prepare but never perform. They wait until they have attained perfection.[52] The house of their friends is ablaze, and

---

[50] Cited in Tugwell, *Early Dominicans*, 240.

[51] Legend has it that six centuries before Humbert's time, my own saintly namesake, Saint Kevin of Glendalough, had to be discovered by a cow as he prayed within the hollow of a tree in his secluded glen of two lakes, and carried off in a litter, at first against his will, for he longed for more contemplation. God had more active plans in mind for him — the founding of what would become a great monastic city. See my *Three Irish Saints* (TAN Books, 2012).

[52] Humbert is so on target here. I have known many well-intentioned people who've sought advice on books they were writing or planning to write, but can count on one hand those who actually submitted them for possible publication (and a few of those led to real books in the papery flesh that can actually be held and read in the other hand!). I knew a person years ago who prepared for a series of scientific talks. The preparation went on and on and almost endlessly, but the talks have not

they delay and do not wake them up. "Run about, make haste, stir up thy friend" (Prov. 6:3). A gloss, Humbert says, relates this to the preacher. Others hold back because of nervousness, laziness, fear of the hardships or poverty, or fear of the hard labors of preaching, a perception of lack of devotion among the people, or because of unsuccessful preaching in the past. Of the last, Humbert asks, "Who ever learned to speak Latin without often speaking bad Latin? Who ever learned to write without frequently writing incorrectly?"[53] Others hold back because they think there are already enough preachers or because they don't like the friar they are paired with in their travels.

All of these excuses are trivial and do not excuse the preacher from preaching. "[P]reach the word, be urgent in season and out of season" (2 Tim. 4:2).

Humbert notes that some who do get out there and preach do so in an undiscriminating manner. They may preach to those who do not want to listen, to those who mean harm to the preacher, to those who are foolish and make light of holy things. Preachers must recall the greatest preacher's advice: "Do not throw your pearls before swine" (Matt. 7:6). Even among those who are inclined to listen, "it is not right to preach the same thing to everybody."[54] The contents of a sermon and its manner of speech must match the ability, character, and needs of the congregation.

---

happened to date. It is good to have good dreams, but we need to wake up and get working to make them come true. Indeed, Humbert's very next line declares that the preacher is called to wake up others too!

[53] Tugwell, *Early Dominicans*, 244.

[54] Ibid., 246.

As for good preaching, Humbert prepares quite a list, and the first item is one uniquely provided by the Order of Preachers. The preacher will ideally have freedom from other responsibilities so that he can devote himself fully to preaching. We see this, for example, in the way, from the very start, religious brothers and others performed supportive tasks of daily living for all the brethren, to free the preaching friars to focus on preaching and on the prayer and study required to sustain it. Humbert cites Saint Paul here on the importance of the pinpointed focus required of the preacher: "Christ did not send me to baptize but to preach the gospel" (1 Cor. 1:17). Saint Dominic himself relaxed the requirements of communal prayer so that friars would have the freedom of which Humbert speaks.

A preacher should also be tranquil and free of disturbance and have a good store of secular knowledge about physics, ethics, logic, and so forth that can be useful in building up the Church, but even more importantly, the preacher must be literally well versed in Scripture! He "should be able to confirm everything he says from scripture."[55] The preacher should mix prayer with his preaching and ask others for their prayers to strengthen him. The preacher needs some periods of rest and leisure, to be spent not in idleness, but in reading, study, and thought that will serve his future preaching. He should be careful about needlessly exposing himself to occasions of sin and should examine his conscience after his travels and preaching, seeking to mend and repair anything broken, like the traveler who cleans his shoes when he arrives at one location, so he is better able to travel on

---

[55] Tugwell, *Early Dominicans*, 251. (Humbert himself does this with his ceaseless citations of Scripture for virtually every point he makes.)

to the next. A preacher must also know how and when to be silent, must keep an awareness of holy love at the forefront of his thoughts, and must always prepare and reflect before preaching.

Good preaching occurs in the places where and for the people whom it is most needed. The prudent traveling preacher does not needlessly upset the local clergy, is not deterred by minor obstacles and setbacks, and must preach "not only with his voice, but with all that he is."[56] He should not only preach to crowds but should also meet with people and exhort them one on one, as Saint Paul did (cf. Acts 20:20, 31). He must also preach with joy and gladness and with confidence and enthusiasm, knowing his strength comes from God.

Indeed, Humbert cites the grace of preaching over other graces. Preaching has advantages over fasting and mortifying the flesh, because it brings discomforts of its own[57] and because it so greatly benefits other people. It has advantages over corporal works of mercy, because although tending to bodily needs is important, even more so is tending to needs of the soul. Indeed, he cites Pope Saint Gregory, who notes that it is better to strengthen minds with the word of God than to fill bellies with earthly bread. Preaching also puts prayer into action, and it is better than sacred reading by itself, because it uses such reading as a means of teaching others. Teaching should be the purpose of reading, and the end or goal is more important than the means. For these reasons and many others I don't have room to include here, Humbert concludes this section with this verse: "Woe is

---

[56] Ibid., 255.

[57] Humbert cites a former monk who said he endured more discomfort in a few days on the road with the Order of Preachers than he had previously dealt with in all of his time at the monastery!

me if I do not preach the gospel. A necessity to preach lies upon me" (1 Cor. 9:16).

How People Come to Lack Preaching

Humbert addresses next the reasons people may come to be without preaching, the characteristics of people who withdraw from preaching, and the harm that results when the gospel is not preached. Sometimes the devil and his minions try to prevent preaching. Sometimes the reason preaching is withheld is known only to God, but sometimes it is good for the people themselves, as when the Holy Spirit prevented preaching in Asia so that wicked men would not receive more severe condemnation because of their hatred of preaching (Acts 16:6). Sometimes it is because of ignorance or indifference among Church leaders or even the actions of some prelates who not only fail to preach, but who work to prevent others from doing so.[58] Lastly, preaching may not issue forth when hearers come only out of curiosity or to be entertained. Here he related a story from the *Lives of the Fathers*. When a group of Brothers and some seculars came out of curiosity to hear Abba Felix, after a long silence he told them that when people come to hear but are not prepared to practice what they hear, God removes the grace of preaching from the elders and they have nothing to say!

Some people may be kept away from preaching by the prompting of the devil, because of human laziness, pride that prevents them from associating with simple people of the crowds, embarrassment that the kinds of sins they indulge in

---

[58] Recall that the Order of Preachers arose partly in response to a dire lack of preaching addressed at the Fourth Lateran Council (1213–1215).

will be brought up in the sermons, busyness in worldly affairs, or because of the silly notion that if one is going to sin, it is better not to know it's a sin, as if purposeful ignorance was itself not sinful! Some wicked souls may actually be afraid they will be prompted to become soft and do good; others are too soft and easy on themselves to hear the hard word of sermons; and others cling to their wickedness like the Pharisees and the lawyers who hardened their hearts against Christ. Woe to them all! "Cursed be the man who does not heed the words of this covenant" (Jer. 11:3).

As for the harm that comes from a lack of preaching, Humbert catalogs a list including the fact that people will remain unbelievers, in error about moral behavior, ignorant of their true selves: "The word of preaching is a kind of mirror, as it says in James 1:23, and people see themselves in it."[59] A dearth of preaching will keep people foolish about what they value and cherish, will bring about a lack of goodness and a growth of evil, as when a lack of nourishing rain ruins good crops and gives rise to thorns, thistles, and weeds. Enemies will exult and the good will remain asleep if the hounds of the Lord and kindred preachers don't alert them to danger and rouse them with the grace of preaching.

The Fruits of Preaching

Humbert begins by quite realistically noting that sometimes there are no fruits at all from good preaching, even for Christ Himself, as we read in John 8:37, "[M]y word finds no place in you." Fishers of men have no guarantee that their fish will not get away! Sometimes preaching has no effect because the hearts of the listeners are like bad soil. Other times it is the preacher's

---

[59] Tugwell, *Early Dominicans*, 266.

fault, due to laziness, a lack of the grace of preaching, or to excessive wordiness.[60]

Humbert then cites another ten reasons why preaching might fail to yield fruit: (1) hardness of heart in the hearer, (2) stupidity of the hearer, (3) rampant wickedness among the people, (4) insensitivity to time and opportunity, (5) too much sensuality, (6) forgetfulness, (7) lack of appetite for the word of God, which is "the mind's food," (8) worldly business, (9) disobedience to a preacher who does not heed his own words, and (10) estrangement from God.

Preaching might produce sour fruits when people don't put into practice what they hear, don't really believe what they hear, laugh at God's message and messengers, or hate and persecute the preachers. Good fruits may come forth that are less than perfect and fall short of ensuring salvation when they instill understanding but not the will to act on it. "Whoever knows what is right to do and fails to do it, for him it is sin" (James 4:17). Another less-than-perfect fruit produces enjoyment and pleasure but does not prompt good acts. Psalm 32:11, after all, says not only, "rejoice," but also, "shout for joy." Sometimes people are stirred emotionally but still do not transform their lives. Hearers of preaching may learn to make critical judgments about the quality of sermons, to praise good preachers, and even learn how to teach, but these are not enough by themselves. Christ said, "Blessed rather are those who hear the word of God and keep it" (Luke 11:28), and Saint Paul said "[Y]ou then who teach others, will you not teach yourself?" (Rom. 2:21).

---

[60] Here again Humbert cites Seneca: "There is no need of many words, but of effective words."

Dominicans know well that as it is better to illuminate than merely to shine reflected light, so too it is better to share the fruits of one's contemplation than simply to contemplate. Preaching is the choice fruit of Dominican contemplation, so what are the fruits of preaching?

Ever thorough, Blessed Humbert lists ten "thoroughly good results of preaching":

- Conversion of unbelievers to a faith in Christ (Acts 11:20–21)

- Conversion of wicked men to repentance (Luke 11:32)

- Conversion of worldly men to humility (1 Kings 21:27)

- Prompting of sinners to go to confession (Matt. 3:5–6)

- Reception of the Holy Spirit (Acts 10:44)

- Sanctification of people from their sins (John 15:3)

- Increase in the Mystical Body of Christ (Acts 2:41)

- Release of the devil's prey (Job 29:17)

- Joy to the angels (Song of Sol. 8:13)

- Defeat of the devil's forces (Judg. 7:22)

Because fruits like these are so important and delectable, Humbert lists a variety of reasons people should listen to preachers when they preach the word of God, and he sums up by stating that listeners should receive God's word with joy, hasten to it, and listen carefully, silently, peacefully, attentively, avidly, patient to the end, and full of devotion.

To put preaching into practice, so consonant with the theme of part 1 of our book, Humbert notes that the hearer of preaching must literally become the doer. "For if any one is a hearer of the word and not a doer, he is like a man who observes his natural face in a mirror; for he observes himself and goes away and at once forgets what he was like" (James 1:23–24).

When the hearer becomes the doer, he becomes a disciple of Christ: "If you continue in my word, you are truly my disciples" (John 8:31). Indeed, they become Christ's friends (John 14:21) and his brother or sister as well (Luke 8:21). The doer obtains God's blessing (Heb. 6:7), is justified (Rom. 2:13), and attains the bliss of beatitude (Luke 11:28).

Other Duties as Assigned

We will quickly round out our treatment of Blessed Humbert on his great treatise on preaching by mentioning in passing what Humbert listed and described in great detail as ten "things that go with the job of preaching" that we might call in modern parlance "other duties as assigned." These include (1) the preacher's travel around the world, (2) his conduct among the people, (3) personal conversations, (4) staying with strangers, (5) involvement in human affairs, (6) requests for advice, (7) hearing confessions, (8) *prothemes*,[61] (9) material for sermons

---

[61] Tugwell, *Early Dominicans*, 325. Citing R. H. and M. A. Rouse's *Preachers: Florilegia and Sermons* (page 73), Tugwell explains that a protheme is "a second text, usually scriptural, allied verbally or logically to the theme itself, and serving as an introduction to remarks upon the necessity of invoking divine aid, which invocation is the purpose and termination of the protheme structure."

and conferences, and (10) prayers that the preacher enjoins on the people.

Rather than fleshing out these ten things with Humbert's own arguments and scriptural references, we will flesh them out in the real flesh-and-blood stories of other real hounds of the Lord. Preaching is so central in various ways to the lives of every one of them that if we pay close attention, we'll see examples aplenty of these and of all kind of duties God assigns to those who take on the habit of the order that Blessed Humbert so deftly and thoroughly helped put in order.

Blessed Humbert's Scriptural Symbols of the Preacher

SYMBOL	SCRIPTURAL PASSAGE
The mouth of the Lord	"If you separate the valuable from the cheap, you will be a kind of mouth for me." (Jer. 15:19)
God's face	"The light of the Lord's face does not fall to the ground." (Job 29:24)
The Lord's feet	"I will honour the place of my feet." (Isa. 60:13)
Angels	"The seven angels prepared themselves to blow the trumpet." (Rev. 8:6)
Eyes, teeth, neck, and breasts of the Church, etc.	Cant. 4:1–5 (Humbert does not supply the complete lengthy passage itself. See the Song of Solomon, or Song of Songs, in the Revised Standard Version, Catholic Edition.)
Heaven	"His Spirit adorned the heavens." (Job 26:13)
Stars	"He enclosed the stars." (Job 9:7)
Doors of heaven	"He ... opened the doors to heaven." (Ps. 78:23)
Clouds	"Clouds give light to everything throughout their course." (cf. Job 37:11–12)

CLARIFYING GLOSS

"Separate: with your words, that is."

"The Church does not preach her radiant mysteries to earthly men."

"Preachers are called the Lord's feet." (cf. Rom. 10:15)

"The whole company of preachers."

Eyes: they watch for hidden things; teeth: they seize the wicked and drag them into the belly of the Church; neck: they supply the breath of life and food of doctrine; breasts: they give milk to the little ones.

"This is glossed 'Preachers.' So the preacher must take care to shine like the sky with all the different virtues which ought to adorn him."

"This is glossed, 'Stars: preachers,' and so they ought to shine on the earth in the darkness of this world, like the stars."

"The doors of heaven are the preachers."

Preachers "enlighten the ends of the world with the light of their preaching."

Blessed Humbert's Scriptural
Symbols of the Preacher

SYMBOL	SCRIPTURAL PASSAGE
Snow	"He commanded the snow to descend upon the earth." (Job 37:6)
Thunder	"When the seven thunders had spoken …" (Apoc. 10:4)
Precious stones	"The king commanded them to bring great stones, precious stones, to set in the foundations of the temple." (3 Kings 5:17)
Mountains	"Let the mountains receive peace for the people, and the hills justice." (Psalm 71:3)
Fountains	"You made the fountains gush forth." (Ps. 73:15)
Eagles	"Wherever there is a corpse, there will soon be an eagle." (Job 39:30)
Cocks	"Who gave the cock understanding?" (Job 39:36)
Ravens	"Who prepared food for the raven, when his little ones cry to God?" (Job 38:41)
Dogs	"Dumb dogs which cannot bark" (Is. 56:10); "They will feel hunger like dogs and go about the city." (Ps. 58:7)
Horses	"Will you give strength to the horse or put his whinnying in his throat?" (Job 39:19)

CLARIFYING GLOSS

"Snow falls from heaven to earth when the lofty minds of the saints, nourished on a contemplation that is well packed and solid, descend to the lowly words of preaching out of love for their brethren."

"They [preachers] are called thunder because it is their job to instill the fear of God."

"The layers of stones which come higher up are the teachers whose preaching makes the church grow and whose virtues adorn her."

"They are the first to receive the bounty of heaven, which they then transmit to places below."

Preachers "pour forth their flow of wisdom."

"A holy preacher flies with eager haste" to bring life to those dead in sin.

Cocks proclaim the light as preachers "crow" by their preaching.

God gives the preacher more than others because He also feeds His chicks with spiritual food.

Barking is preaching. The preacher wanders about like a hungry dog and "swallows up souls into the body of the church."

The horse is the preacher who receives strength by conquering his own vice and his whinnying is his preaching to educate others.

Blessed Humbert's Scriptural
Symbols of the Preacher

SYMBOL	SCRIPTURAL PASSAGE
Oxen	"A thousand yoke of oxen" (Job 42:12); "Where there are no oxen, the manger is empty. Where there is an abundant harvest to be seen, it proves the strength of the oxen." (Prov. 14:4)
Standard bearers of the army of the king of heaven	"Lift up a sign for the people." (Isa. 62:10)
Messengers of Ahaseurus	"King Ahasuerus sent letters throughout all the provinces of his realm." (Esther 1:22)
Strong men of David	"I have called my strong men in my wrath." (Isa. 13:3)
Officers of Solomon	"The officers, with immense care, supplied what was needed for the table of King Solomon at the appropriate time." (3 Kings 4:27)
Bricklayers	"They gave money to bricklayers." (Ezra 3:7)
Watchmen of the House of Israel	"Son of man, I have appointed you watchman to the house of Israel." (Ezek. 3:17)

CLARIFYING GLOSS

The oxen are the preachers who should work hard in the fields to show their strength.

The sign is the cross of the Passion and Resurrection, lifted up by preaching.

He sent out instructions and rebukes through his preachers.

The gloss gives Paul as an example. As the text goes on, "The Lord of hosts has given the word to the army which fights this war," the gloss notes the preachers are given the armor of the apostles.

The order of preachers labors in writing and speech to make provision in the Lord's house to nourish all the faithful.

The preachers build men up in good works and bind them in charity, as if putting together cut and polished stones to uphold the whole construction.

A preacher's way of life should set him up high, so he can be useful by seeing into the distance.

Saint Hyacinth of Poland

1185–1257 | FEAST: AUGUST 17

Having so recently benefited from the long and happy pontificate of our first Polish pontiff, Saint John Paul II, we are well poised to honor the Apostle to the North, who evangelized Poland and much of northeastern Europe. The learned priest and theological doctor Hyacinth was born in Kraków and educated at Bologna and Paris. While in Rome in 1218, he was so moved by his encounter with Saint Dominic that he joined the Dominican Order and within a few months returned to Kraków with Saint Ceslaus (probably his brother) and two others, commencing to found and lead new Dominican convents there. Saint Hyacinth would later evangelize and spread the gospel into many countries to the north and east of Poland, in spite of the many dangers of the time. So powerful was Hyacinth's zeal to save souls that he was said to have obtained Saint Dominic's spirit when he donned the Dominican habit. An indefatigable doer, he was said to have logged nearly twenty-five thousand miles (roughly the circumference of the earth) in his zeal to save souls by bringing them to Christ.

Like his spiritual father Dominic, Saint Hyacinth had a special devotion to Mary. The story is told that while in a church in Kiev, in the midst of a Tartar invasion, he grabbed the monstrance containing the Blessed Sacrament to carry it to safety when he heard a female voice say in effect, "Take me too!" He was then able to hoist onto his shoulders a massive alabaster statue of the Virgin Mary, far exceeding what his normal strength could carry, thus saving her image as well. Saint Hyacinth received a warning on the eve of the Assumption that his death was near. He said Mass as a dying man on August 15, 1257, and on that date this great Pole and Dominican began his life in heaven.

Blessed Fra Angelico
and the Art of Doing

> *Every art is so constituted that it is a habit, concerned with making, under the guidance of reason. Likewise, no productive habit of this kind, i.e., directed by reason, is found which is not an art. Hence, it is evident that art is the same as a habit concerned with making under the guidance of true reason.*
> —Saint Thomas Aquinas, *Commentary on Aristotle's Nichomachean Ethics*
>
> *But it is impossible to bestow too much praise on this holy father, who was so humble and modest in all that he did and said and whose pictures were painted with such facility and piety.*
> —Giorgio Vasari, *Lives of the Artists*
>
> *To paint Christ, one must live Christ.*
> —Fra Angelico

Preaching in Living Color

There is a saying often attributed to Saint Dominic's friend and brother in Christ, Saint Francis of Assisi, that runs, "Preach the gospel always; if necessary, use words." Surely everyone has also heard that "a picture is worth a thousand words." Whether he had heard these sayings or not, the man who would become known as Fra Angelico, the Angelic Friar, *lived* them like few men before him or since! His pictures literally preach the gospels. And if a picture is truly worth a thousand words, the extent of his preaching rivals the worth of the wordiest of theologians, that other great Dominican who was compared to the angels, Saint Thomas Aquinas, the Angelic Doctor.

The Angelic Doctor's quotation on the nature of art declared that any kind of making is a *habit*, or a refined skill guided by reason. Fra Angelico had unquestionably employed his powers of reason to master the art of painting. Saint Thomas notes as well, though, that God bestows gifts that surpass the powers of reason alone. The gifts of the Holy Spirit, for example, enable us to function not merely in accordance with the dictates of reason but in accordance with the Holy Spirit's guidance. Twentieth-century Dominican Thomist Father Réginald Garrigou-Lagrange wrote that natural virtues are like the oars with which we row to truth and goodness, whereas the Holy Spirit's gifts are like the winds beneath our sails. Anyone who has even glanced at a work of Fra Angelico will sense that he did not just "row" those paintings into existence. God's gifts undoubtedly billowed those sails, taking Fra Angelico to the most heavenly of destinations.

Let's take a quick look at the holy man behind the holy art.

A Brief Portrait of Fra Angelico

Estimates of the year of birth of Guido da Vicchio[62] vary from 1386 to 1395. The "da Vicchio" tells us that he was born in the

---

[62] Some sources name him Guido di Pietro, referring to his father, named Pietro. He was also known in his day as John of Fiesole.

town of Vicchio, about sixteen miles northeast of Florence, in the rich, verdant lands of northern Italy. Although details of his early life are very sparse, we know that young Guido (or Guidolino, "little Guido") had an older brother Benedetto, a Dominican priest who was also an artist and who is known mostly for his miniatures, especially his artistic illumination of sacred books.[63]

We know that Guido was drawn to the religious life as a young man, and he resided at the Dominican convent in Cortona, sixty miles or so southeast of Florence, from 1408 to 1418. By 1423 he had become a Dominican priest, as he was known from that time by his new religious name: Fra (Friar) Giovanni (John). He resided at the Dominican convent at Fiesole, Italy, at the northeast edge of Florence, a house of Conventual, or "Observant," Dominicans, a branch within the Order of Preachers that strove to return to some of the order's more austere and primitive roots but remained in unity with the rest of the order. He lived there from 1418 to 1436.

Then Fra Giovanni moved to the Friary of San Marco (Saint Mark) in Florence, where he would stay, paint extensively, and serve as prior until 1445, when Pope Eugenius IV called him to Rome to paint the Chapel of the Holy Sacrament at Saint Peter's.

In 1447, at the pope's request, he headed to Orvieto, with his student Benozzo Gozzoli, to paint the vaulted ceiling of the Capella Nuova (New Chapel) in the magnificent cathedral. They

---

[63] Anyone who has seen samples of illuminated sacred books, such as the famous Books of Kells in Dublin, Ireland, can almost lament the rise of the printing press, which led to the demise of such colorful, ornate, and intricate book decoration. Sister Dorcy reports that Benedetto painted and illuminated a set of choir books that were "reputed to be the loveliest in the world." Sister Mary Jean Dorcy, *Saint Dominic's Family*, 201.

painted a scene of *Christ in Judgment,* and another of *Angels and Prophets.* He then took commissions from Pope Nicholas V for his own Niccoline Chapel, a private chapel in the Vatican dedicated to Saints Stephen and Lawrence. That vault featured stunningly colorful images of the four evangelists in their traditional symbols of the four winged creatures described in Ezekiel 10 and Revelation 4, showing Saint Mark with a lion, Saint Matthew with a man, Saint Luke with a bull, and Saint John with an eagle.[64]

Fra Angelico would return to Fiesole and serve as prior there for three years, from 1449 to 1452, until he was called back to Rome in 1454. He died in 1455, somewhere in his sixties, at the Dominican convent at the Santa Maria Sopra Minerva,[65] probably while working for Pope Nicholas V. He was buried in that church, and the inscription under his marble monument reads (in translation of the Latin):

[64] Some have noted that among the reasons for the particular associations are the facts that Saint Mark emphasizes Christ's kingship, Saint Matthew emphasizes His human genealogy and His Incarnation, Saint Luke begins his Gospel with a sacrifice, and Saint John's Gospel teaches the highest theology of God's divinity (like the eagle, which was believed to be able to look straight into the sun).

[65] The church still exists a block from the ancient pagan Pantheon (temple to "all gods" — now the Catholic Church of Saint Mary and the Martyrs) and was built on the site of another ancient pagan temple, believed now to have been dedicated to the Egyptian goddess Isis, but long believed to have been dedicated to the Roman goddess Minerva, so the name of the Church, from the original Latin, Sanctae Mariae supra Minvervam, means "Saint Mary over Minerva." For a time it was headquarters (convent and studium) to the Dominicans, who have since returned to their original Roman home of the Basilica of Santa Sabina.

Give me not praise for being almost a second
    Appelles,[66] *but because I*
Gave to the poor, O Christ, all my earnings.
    Thus part of my work remains
On earth and part in heaven. My home was in
    that city, which is the
Flower of Etruria.[67]

The biographer Giorgio Vasari, a sixteenth-century Italian painter, architect, and historian, praises Fra Angelico's holy character in the highest terms. He said that Fra Angelico could have been rich through his painting but chose the simple, holy life of chastity, obedience, and poverty within the Dominican Order. Vasari relates that the artist had scruples of conscience one morning at breakfast with the pope himself (Nicholas V), fearing to eat the meat that was offered to him without his prior's permission (forgetting for a time about the authority of the man who had offered it to him!). Vasari also reports that Fra Angelico turned down the pope's offer of an archbishopric, believing an abler man deserved the seat (the future Dominican later known as Saint Antoninus) and because he knew that God had called him to paint.

Fra Angelico was described as kindly and temperate, of "incredible sweetness," and was never seen angry at his fellow friars. If a friend should need correction, Fra Angelico would

---

[66] Apelles of Kos, an ancient (fourth century B.C.) Greek artist, considered by some the greatest of all.

[67] Cited in J. B. Supino, *Fra Angelico*, trans. Leader Scott (Florence: Alinari Brothers, n.d.); available at Project Gutenberg, accessed August 22, 2015, http://www.gutenberg.org/files/21561/21561-h/21561-h.htm.

offer it with a simple smile. Vasari opined that no man had ever painted more saintly saints, more angelic angels, or more heavenly images of heaven, and this was possible only because of Fra Angelico's own holy devotion to God. Once a painting was complete, Fra Angelico never went back to retouch or enhance it, believing it was God's will to leave it as it was.

Unfortunately, the ravages of history have not left all of this great Dominican's works completely as they were, and some have suffered significant damage over the last five centuries and more. Far more fortunately, though, history has preserved a great abundance of his works, and many in excellent shape. To do justice to this great blessed, and to the special talent with which he was blessed by God, I will attempt to describe as best as I can in words a sample of the works that Vasari proclaimed "so beautiful that words are not able to describe them."

Since the Dominicans so love the Rosary and are so connected with its development, I'll use the mysteries of the Rosary to highlight a small fraction of Fra Angelico's angelic art. The *Catechism of the Catholic Church* relates that the Rosary is an "epitome of the whole Gospel" (CCC 971). An epitome is an especially representative summary, and the gospel is what the hounds of the Lord lived to preach. Here, then, is a Rosary-based epitome of the Gospel-based art of the preacher with a paintbrush, Blessed Fra Angelico.

The Joyous Mysteries of Fra Angelico

The Annunciation. The First Joyful Mystery of the Rosary is the Annunciation, that glorious moment when the angel Gabriel announced God's most amazing request to the Holy Virgin Mary, that she should bear His own Son, and she responded with that incredible yes: "Behold, I am the handmaid of the Lord; let it be to me according to your word" (Luke 1:38). Through the centuries, countless artists have depicted this serene yet earth-shaking scene, and thanks be to God, Fra Angelico did so several times and I'll mention just a few.[68]

From around 1430 to 1432 Fra Angelico worked, using tempera,[69] on an altarpiece depicting the Annunciation for the Church of San Domencio in his town of Fiesole. One is struck in this work, as in all of Fra Angelico's works, by the astonishingly vibrant colors. The angel Gabriel and the Virgin Mary are clad in a pinkish hue, and Mary is covered by a rich dark-blue cape. Both figures have fair skin and blond hair, and a golden ray of light descends from the sky to the left over the head of the bowing angel and onto the Holy Virgin, serenely leaning forward with her arms folded across her chest. She sits in an open porch, and to the left we see another angel expelling Adam and Eve from the Garden of Eden. Mary will be the New Eve who will

---

[68] On a thankful note at the personal level: as I began my research on Fra Angelico for this book in March of 2015, upon walking into the offices of a Saint Francis of Assisi Church in the heart of Texas, the first work of art to catch my eye was a large-scale reproduction of one of Fra Angelico's Annunciations — the one for San Domenico in Cortona, I believe.

I would encourage readers while or after reading this chapter to track down, examine, and meditate on images of Fra Angelico's artworks through art books, the Internet, or other sources. My primary source is Gabriele Bartz's coffee-table book in the *Masters of Italian Art* series, *Fra Angelico* (Koln, Germany: Konemann Verlagsgesellschaft, 1998).

[69] Commonly used before the advent of oil-based painting, tempera consisted of dyes mixed with a water-soluble binder, such as egg yolk, egg, or milk.

make way for the redemption of man's sins through the Child she will bear.

Although a total amateur when it comes to art, I will admit I am struck by the way in which Fra Angelico depicts the grand, majestic wings of the angels in his many Annunciations. In this one, they appear highly textured with different shades of brown, highlighted by red and gold.

A few years later (1432–1434), Fra Angelico produced another Annunciation on a panel for another Church of San Domenico, this one in Cortona, Italy. The scene has many similarities to the one at Fiesole, but in this one, the angel's pink garments are more vibrant, and Mary's dress a more striking red. Here too, the words of the Annunciation are depicted in gold, flowing back and forth between Gabriel and Mary, perhaps recalling how the paintings and statues within medieval churches were themselves tools for preaching and teaching. Here too Gabriel is particularly striking, with a rich golden halo and grand, textured wings of gold highlighted with hues of brown and red. A similar altarpiece was done around 1440 for a convent of San Francesco, again with unique twists of its own, and with, as the others, a predella[70] below depicting scenes from the life of the Virgin Mary.

A last Annunciation I'll mention is a fresco[71] at the Dominican Convent of San Marco in Florence.[72] Completed in 1450,

---

[70] A predella is a frame of several small pictures that run along the bottom of an altarpiece.

[71] Fresco is a technique in which an artist paints a mural directly on wet plaster using pigments made with water. The painting and the plaster dry together so that the mural becomes embedded in the wall, has a matte finish, and is very durable. Interestingly, the color changes as it dries, so the artist must anticipate the finished hues.

[72] This convent houses the present-day Museum of San Marco.

this fresco "has come to mean the very essence of Fra Angelico's art. It is framed as though it were a view into another world."[73] It is simpler and less adorned than the previously mentioned Annunciations, and what strikes this amateur most is the beauty of Mary's countenance, and the strikingly rich colors of Gabriel's wings in rows of gold, pink, white, aquamarine, red, and black.

The Visitation. Due to the confines of space, I'll mention only one or two of Fra Angelico's paintings of the other mysteries of the Rosary. In the predella of the Annunciation at Cortona we find a painting of the Visitation. Mary, in red and blue, greets her cousin Elizabeth, dressed in black and white at a house atop a hill. Two servants are depicted as well, and off in the distance Fra Angelico has depicted a realistic landscape, not of the Holy Land, but of the view from Cortona of Lake Trasimeno and of the town Castiglione del Lago. The predella includes other scenes, including the wedding of the Virgin, the adoration of the Magi, the Presentation in the Temple, and the death of the Virgin.

The Nativity. A beautiful Nativity scene includes in a three-by-three grouping of scenes that are among the thirty-five that Fra Angelico painted around 1450 to adorn the door panels of a silver cabinet for the Santissima Annunziata in Florence. His depiction looks like a beautiful version of a modern Christmas crèche, the holy Infant on the ground of a stable, with a kneeling Mary and Joseph praying over him, and a group of six angels praying on the roof.

The Presentation. The aforementioned panel of paintings at Cortona featuring the Visitation also includes a depiction of the Presentation. One sees inside the nave of the Temple as Simeon,

[73] Bartz, *Masters of Italian Art: Fra Angelico*, 82.

bedecked in gold, caresses the golden Christchild and Joseph, Mary, and Anna look on.

The Finding of the Child Jesus in the Temple. In the bottom-right panel of the door for the cabinet in Florence mentioned above, we find the youthful Jesus seated with holy writ in His lap, opening the Scriptures for the rabbis at the Temple, as Joseph and Mary walk in from the left, the Holy Family alone crowned with halos.

The Luminous Mysteries of Fra Angelico

The Baptism of Jesus. Cell 24 at San Marco in Florence contains *The Baptism of Christ.* In the center is Christ, standing in a blue-green River Jordan, clad in white loincloth, hands folded in prayer. Saint John the Baptist, one foot on a rock and the other submerged in the river, baptizes the haloed Christ, pouring water from a bowl. Above Christ in a cloud is the Holy Spirit in the form of a white dove. At the bottom left, two golden-haired angels are kneeling and holding Christ's garments for Him. At the bottom right are the Virgin Mary and Saint Dominic, who holds a book of the Scriptures in one hand and a lily in the other.

The Wedding at Cana. In a panel for the silver chest at San Marco, Fra Angelico (in 1452) painted a festive Wedding at Cana. Beneath a blue and red checkerboard pattern sit Jesus and the Virgin Mary next to the newly married couple as well as another man and woman. In front of the table, one young golden-haired servant fills a set of blue vessels, while another addresses the guests.

The Proclamation of the Kingdom. Cell 32 at San Marco houses Fra Angelico's stunning *Sermon on the Mount.* This painting is one of many clear examples of why Fra Angelico is considered a master of light and of color, as well as a spiritual master. Near the top of a stylized mountain Jesus sits with right hand raised, teaching a semicircle of twelve apostles. Jesus' garments are in pastels of pink, purple, and maroon, with a border of aquamarine. The apostles are arrayed in a veritable rainbow of colors. The most striking feature of all, however, is a beautiful gold-yellow glow that illuminates the rock of the mountain in the space that Jesus and His apostles enclose. Christ was, after all, proclaiming a kingdom that was not of this world, but which one enters into even on earth by accepting His invitation.[74]

The Transfiguration. Cell 6 is home to *The Transfiguration of Christ.* Here, in this meeting of heaven and earth, a haloed Christ, clad in white, stands on a rock, His body surrounded by a white oval. To His left and His right, the faces of Moses and Elijah look upon Him, while below on the earth a startled Peter, James, and John look on, with the prayerful Blessed Virgin to their left and the prayerful Saint Dominic to their right.

The Institution of the Eucharist. Our last stop in this tour of the mysteries of the Rosary is cell 35 at San Marco, where we find *The Institution of the Eucharist* (circa 1450). As we peer into this room, we see two rooms, as it were. Two windows above the table depict that actual view outside the windows into the opposite cloister at San Marco, while an open door shows a courtyard with a well. Of far greater interest is the much older room where this great mystery actually took place. Christ stands outside a long L-shaped table, presenting the Eucharist to a young clean-shaven apostle (perhaps John?). Eight apostles sit behind the

---

[74] And, of course, as all Dominicans know, "it is better to enlighten than merely to shine."

table, while off to the right four more kneel with folded hands in prayer, as if waiting to receive the Eucharist as it was received in medieval times. A unique feature of this painting is the kneeling Virgin Mother at the bottom left. The picture is colorful, as always, with main themes of light brown and dark red, suggesting perhaps the body and blood of Christ.

The Sorrowful Mysteries of Fra Angelico

The Agony in the Garden. A gorgeous fresco in cell 34 at the Church (and now museum) of San Marco in Florence, from around 1450, shows a kneeling, praying Christ conversing with an angel, while down the hill, Saints James, John, and Peter sleep in various postures, and on the other side of a wall Saints Martha and Mary are immersed in holy reading and prayer. In another scene from around the same time on the panel of the silver chest in Florence, the apostles sleep while Jesus prays with an angel. The women are not present, and the garden is embellished with detailed foliage of springtime.

The Scourging at the Pillar. *The Flagellation*, from around 1441, in cell 27 in the Museum of San Marco, depicts Christ bound to a pillar, with a golden halo with a red cross upon his head. The mourning Virgin Mary, deep in prayer, turns her head away from Christ, while a barebacked Saint Dominic looks up at Christ and strikes his own back with a whip of cords, suffering in sympathy with Christ.[75]

The Crowning with Thorns. *The Mockery of Christ*, from around 1441, appears in cell 7 of the same museum in Florence. Here,

---

[75] A depiction of the penitential discipline involved in Saint Dominic's own "third way" of prayer.

depicted with both a heavenly crown of a halo and an earthly crown of sharp thorns, a blindfolded Christ sits surrounded by symbols of insult, such as the head of a spitting man and hands ready to slap Him and to strike Him with a stick. Again, to the lower left sits the mourning Virgin, and to the right a serene Saint Dominic looks down at the text of the Gospel, meditating on this most sorrowful scene.

The Carrying of the Cross. In cell 28, also from around 1441, is *Christ Carrying the Cross.* Bedecked in red, Christ looks ahead as He carries His Cross, His Mother Mary behind Him, hands folded in prayer, and kneeling before Him with a Gospel text on the ground, Saint Dominic gazes upon Him, His hands also crossed in prayer.

The Crucifixion. As we come to the literal crux of these mysteries, and indeed, of salvation history, you can rest assured that Fra Angelico applied his great skills to depict the Crucifixion many times. I'll describe only one. The massive fresco of *The Crucifixion* from 1441 to 1442 takes up the entire back wall of the Dominican chapter room at the Church of San Marco in Florence. Here we find Christ on His Cross flanked by the two thieves as a bevy of saints gaze upon Him in prayer.[76] Curving across from bottom left to bottom right is a large border with depictions of patriarchs and prophets, and across the bottom are seventeen small, round medallion portraits of prominent Dominicans.

---

[76] These saints include John the Baptist, Mark, Lawrence, Dominic, Jerome, Ambrose, Augustine, Benedict, Bernard of Clairvaux, Francis of Assisi, Thomas Aquinas, and several others.

The Glorious Mysteries of Fra Angelico

The Resurrection. Cell 8 at San Marco contains *The Resurrection*, circa 1441. Four saintly women in reds, purples, browns, and greens, who have come to wash Christ's body, stand at right and center, but the white sarcophagus is empty. Sitting in a leisurely pose on the lip of one corner, an angel clad in white points upward to the risen Christ. Above the women and invisible to them is Christ, clad in white, with a golden halo with a red cross, surrounded by a golden oval emitting rays of light, and with a group of clouds rising to a bit above knee level. He holds a palm in His right hand and, in His left, a pole with a white banner containing a red cross. Tucked away in the lower left corner is a man with a golden halo with a red star on top. He is clad in black and white, kneeling in prayer with his hands folded across his chest. This is, of course, Saint Dominic meditating on the risen Savior.

The panel of the silver chest at San Marco also contains a Resurrection scene. Here five haloed women in striking reds, yellows, and blues gaze in awe at Christ's open tomb. On each side of the entrance is a palm tree. Inside the cave is a golden-winged angel telling the women the good news of the Resurrection.

The Ascension. In a panel painting for the silver chest we also find one of Fra Angelico's Ascensions. Here, in a serene natural landscape with green trees nearby and hills in the distance, Mary, in blue and white, kneels, hands folded in prayer, at the center of a circle of colorful apostles in blues, reds, pinks, greens, and yellows, accompanied by two angels just outside their circle. Above the Blessed Virgin in the sky is the bottom edge of a golden disc, revealing white clouds and the bottom of Christ's white robe.

In another *Ascension*, this one featured in a triptych panel (along with the Last Judgment and Pentecost), is a more closely cropped circle of apostles, Blessed Mary at the center, hands folded in prayer, and a white-robe Christ hovers above them. Here there are no elements of nature. The background is nothing but majestic, shimmering gold.

The Descent of the Holy Spirit. On the panel of the silver chest at San Marco is a depiction of Pentecost by Fra Angelico. Twenty-six disciples are gathered in the Upper Room of Acts 1 and 2 with the Virgin Mary at their center. They appear as if in a balcony, so the viewer can see into the room, as if from above. Only the heads of the disciples can be seen, but Blessed Mary, clad in dark blue, is visible from the waist up. Her hands are folded in prayer. On her golden halo and on those of the disciples is a bright red tongue of flame.[77] Below the level of the Upper Room we see outside a group of five Jews gathered from different parts of the world who find they are able to understand each other's tongues, in a spillover of the great miracle.[78]

The Assumption of Mary. *The Dormition and Assumption of the Virgin* was completed in Florence around 1432, and words cannot begin to do it justice, both for the beauty of its golden background and the richest of blues, and for its striking emotional and devotional impact. In a bottom panel, the Virgin rests on her back on a funeral bier, surrounded by apostles, four of whom are about to carry her to her tomb. Her holy Son stands in the

[77] "And there appeared to them tongues as of fire, distributed and resting on each one of them" (Acts 2:3).
[78] "And they were all filled with the Holy Spirit and began to speak in other tongues, as the Spirit gave them utterance" (Acts 2:4).

center, holding an infant that symbolizes His acceptance of His mother's soul. In the scene right above it, Mary, now standing in garb of light blue and gold, rises through the clouds accompanied by three tiers of colorful angels, the first tier kneeling in prayer, the next tier standing around her, and the third, highest tier playing musical instruments for a heavenly choir. The background is in majestic gold, and above the Virgin Mary, Christ, in the richest of blues, reaches down to receive His Mother, with images of the Father and the Holy Spirit, all in blue, merging into His image behind Him.

The Coronation of the Queen of Heaven. We are blessed that Fra Angelico addressed the crowning of Mary many times in many paintings still extant, indeed one of them at the Louvre in France. While readers are encouraged to track down, examine, and meditate on them all, space will permit the detailed description of but one. *The Coronation of the Virgin*, now at the Uffizi Museum in Florence, is as majestic as can be. This tempera painting on a wooden panel dazzles the eye with its light and its rich, golden background. Sitting high in the center, on a bank of clouds, a radiant Christ crowns the head of his radiant Mother, Mary. Angels surround them, blaring out with trumpets standing as high as the angels are tall. They are joined all around in a great circle extending to the bottom, still in a realm of the clouds, by dozens of recognizable saints from different eras and lands, gazing in various directions. In a particularly striking feature near the bottom to the right of the center, a pensive, golden-haired Saint Mary Magdalene peers out at the painting's viewer.

As we end this tour of the Rosary's mysteries, let me strongly suggest taking time to look at these and other paintings by Blessed Fra Angelico and using them as devotional aids when praying the Rosary. It can add an "Angelic" dimension to this holy prayer so dear to the hounds of the Lord.

The Hounds of the Lord and Their Next of Kin

So many Fra Angelico masterpieces, and so little time and space to describe them! I'll end this chapter by noting that this gifted son of Saint Dominic has painted a vast number of moving scenes in addition to those found in the Rosary mysteries we reviewed. Particularly noteworthy are his many glorious paintings of the Madonna and Child.

Some also consider his *Last Judgment*, a tempera painting on panel at San Marco, among his most intricate and magnificent works. It has an odd shape, like a long, low rectangle with three semi-circles at the top, because it was designed to be used as the back of the incredibly ornate chair the priest would use at Mass. To the left of center we find groups of angels, of patriarchs, of prophets, and of saints of all times and places experiencing great joy as they peer at Christ elevated in the center, having judged that they shall enter heaven. Below to the right is a much different, much darker, and quite chaotic scene. To the right of center beastly demons herd people toward hell, some of whom are clad in religious garments, even mitered bishops and cardinal-red cardinals. The far right shows seven groups of the damned, naked, suffering various torments befitting their various sins. At the very bottom, in the center of the bowels of hell, is a horned, beastly Satan, devouring people whole. Some commentators have noted, by the way, that the figures on the right are very simply drawn, while the figures above and to the left are richly and beautifully drawn. Vasari said that the angelic Fra Angelico was uncomfortable using his artistic gifts to portray scenes of ugliness and evil.

I'll conclude our brief chapter on this incredibly blessed artistic doer by noting how many of his paintings also directly depict or include a vast array of the Church's Communion of Saints up to Angelico's time. A great patron of San Marco (Saint Mark's Cathedral), for example, was the wealthy and powerful Cosimo de Medici, who essentially ruled Florence for a time. The patrons of the Medici family were the twin Saints Cosmas (or Cosimo) and Damian, third-century physicians who were martyred. The predella for Fra Angelico's great altarpiece at San Marco includes scenes from the lives of these martyrs, and in one striking scene, Saint Damian turns to the Virgin to pray, while Saint Cosmas, resplendent in red and gold, turns to look out directly at the viewer.

Fra Angelico's greatest patrons and dearest friends of all, of course, were his Dominican brothers and sisters. Various hounds of the Lord, and their master, Saint Dominic himself, appear in countless numbers in Fra Angelico's paintings. Among the most striking at San Marco depicts a detailed kneeling Saint Dominic looking up at Christ on the Cross. Dominic clutches the wood underneath Christ's pierced feet as blood trails from between each toe all the way to the ground. Dominic's agony and love are quite palpable.

As religious brothers entered San Marco, they were greeted by a painting of Saint Peter Martyr, quill and book in his left hand, his index finger held up over his lip, producing the world's most beautiful "No talking!" sign. This saint appears in many of Angelico's works. He is recognizable by the bloody crown on his head, representing where he was martyred by the strike of an ax.

Saint Thomas Aquinas is also frequently to be found, and interestingly enough, Saint Francis of Assisi too, demonstrating the reverence for their founders and the goodwill between the twin mendicant orders of the Friars Preachers and the Friars Minor. *The Crucifixion* and *The Coronation of the Virgin* are examples of two paintings at San Marco that feature, as if they were present, Saints Dominic, Peter Martyr, Thomas Aquinas, and Francis all together, along with many more saints who lived long before either order existed.

So simple, holy, devout, and talented was Fra Giovanni that he earned the unofficial titles or nicknames of Blessed and Angelico while he was still alive. On February 18, 1455, while in Rome at the service of our 208th pontiff, Nicholas V, Giovanni's life on earth ended and his life in heaven began. Fifty-six popes and 527 years later, on October 3, 1982, Pope Saint John Paul II declared the official beatification of Blessed Fra Angelico, stating:

> Angelico was reported to say, "He who does Christ's work must stay with Christ always." This motto earned him the epithet "Blessed Angelico," because of the perfect integrity of his life and the almost divine beauty of the images he painted, to a superlative extent those of the Blessed Virgin Mary.

Two years later, John Paul II named him the patron of Catholic artists. We need not be artists, of course, to experience the blessings of Blessed Fra Angelico. (If you have yet to stop and take a look and meditate on some pieces of his holy art, please take this as your cue, and I doubt you'll be disappointed!)

Saint Agnes of Montepulciano

1268–1357 | FEAST: APRIL 20

Saint Agnes of Rome (c. 291–c. 304) was a young virgin martyr who refused to disavow her devotion to Christ regardless of the consequences. One hound of the Lord, Saint Thomas Aquinas, carried a relic of her on his person, and another, Saint Agnes of Montepulciano, carried her name and in her own youth did great things for Lord.

In the small Tuscan village of Gracciano Vecchio, Agnes's birth was announced by mysterious lights surrounding the house where she was born. By the time she was six, she began asking her parents for permission to enter a convent. By the time she was nine, she was permitted to enter a Franciscan convent in nearby Montepulciano. The nuns were known as Sisters of the Sack for their rough-hewn garments and their simple prayer-filled lives in the pattern of Saint Francis of Assisi, their spiritual father. Here this contemplative soul soon became a doer as well, being named bursar of the convent before the age of fifteen. She was then called to a convent in Procena, where she served as prioress for the next twenty years. Then, inspired by a vision of Saint Dominic one day, she would go on to found a new convent of the Dominican Order in Montepulciano, starting it with three stones given to her by the Blessed Mother.

Many miracles are attributed to Saint Agnes, from a chance to hold the infant Jesus to the restoration of the life of a young child who had drowned. When first installed as an abbess, tiny white crosses rained down on the church like manna from heaven. Blessed Raymond of Capua, biographer of Saint Agnes and of Saint Catherine of Siena, reports that when Saint Catherine visited Saint Agnes's incorrupt remains and bent down to kiss her foot, Agnes obliged, and her foot rose to meet Catherine's lips!

PART 2

Dominican Thinkers and the Contemplative Style

By wisdom a house is built,
and by understanding it is established;
by knowledge the rooms are filled
with all precious and pleasant riches.
—Proverbs 24:3–4

Saint Albert the Great Enlightens Us with Science

For from the greatness and beauty of created things
comes a corresponding perception of their Creator.
—Wisdom 13:5

Almost, we can say, like a first Adam on the earth, in the
middle of the thirteenth century Albert of Cologne began to look
at the world around him with a completely fresh gaze. In his
commentary on Matthew's Gospel he wrote: "The whole world is
theology for us because the heavens proclaim the glory of God."
—Paul Murray, O.P.,
The New Wine of Dominican Spirituality

Saintly Scientist

Born on earth around 1200 and in heaven in 1280, Saint Albert
the Great of the Order of Preachers is a great saint for *our* time
so badly in need of his preaching and teaching.[79] We live in a

---

[79] When people ask me for my favorite saint, I sometimes say that
   if I could write a complete biography on only one saint, I'm

world where many scientists proclaim their lack of belief in God and increasing numbers of young people declare they believe in science rather than religion, assuming in the ignorance of their miseducation that the two must be opposed. As Pope Saint John Paul II declared in 1998 in his *Fides et Ratio* (on the relationship between faith and reason), we live in a day when *scientism* grows rampant and many people believe that science and technology provide all the answers to all the problems that plague humanity. On the other hand, some Christians who recognize that science can certainly tell us *how* to do things, but not whether we *ought* to do them, fall into the opposing error of *fideism*, "which fails to recognize the importance of rational knowledge and philosophical discourse for the understanding of faith, indeed for the very possibility of belief in God."[80] We live in a day of increasing polarization, presented with the false dichotomy of having to choose between the scientism of the intelligent, courageous, and godless secular scientists and the fideism of ignorant, benighted, and bigoted fundamentalist Bible-thumpers.

The Catholic Church, however, has never been the Church of either-or but of both-and insofar as there are kernels of truth in each side. John Paul II in our time would describe faith and reason as the "two wings on which the human spirit rises to

---

pretty sure it would be Saint Albert the Great. Actually, I'm certain, because I've written only one biography so far, and it was indeed on Saint Albert—*Saint Albert the Great: Champion of Faith and Reason* (TAN Books, 2011). I bring this up because many of the themes addressed in brief in this chapter are explored in more depth in that book, so those who'd care for more on the life of this great saint are most cordially invited to go there as well.

[80] John Paul II, *Fides et Ratio*, no. 55.

the contemplation of truth."[81] And among the Catholic faithful throughout the centuries, few have embraced and proclaimed the inherent harmony of science and faith, of reason and revelation, like our hounds of the Lord, true champions of faith and reason, the sons and daughters of Saint Dominic de Guzman.

On November 15, 1980, eighteen years before he released *Fides et Ratio*, the same saintly pope previewed some of his profound thoughts on the fundamental complementarity of faith and reason in a speech in Cologne, Germany. The occasion was the seven hundredth anniversary of the death of none other than Saint Albert the Great. John Paul II praised Albert for his virtue of *courage* in championing man's reason as a grand instrument to find truth and to shape and structure the world, and also for his virtue of *humility* to recognize reason's limits and remain "open to the Word of eternal Truth, which became man in Christ."[82]

Almost thirty years later, in an address on March 24, 2010, Saint John Paul II's successor, Pope Benedict XVI, would again recommend to us the virtues of Saint Albert, portraying Albert (named the patron saint of scientists by Pope Pius XII in 1941) as a model for modern scientists to follow in transforming the study of nature into a fulfilling and "fascinating journey of holiness." Indeed, Pope Benedict spoke of the "friendship" of reason and faith, of Saint Albert's realization that reason and Scripture are completely compatible, and of God's will that we are to use both to seek and attain truth and happiness.

Approaching six years later, as we anticipate the eight hundredth Jubilee of the Orders of Preachers on December 22, 2016,

---

[81] Ibid., preamble.

[82] John Paul II, *Science and Faith in the Search of Truth*, Caltech Newman Center, accessed August 22, 2015, http://www.its. caltech.edu/~nmcenter/sci-cp/sci80111.html.

we need the model and lessons of Saint Albert even more as the world questions and "deconstructs" moral and existential truths that seemed to be settled ages ago. "What does it mean to be a man or a woman?" "What is the nature of marriage?" "Do things really have identities or natures of their own, or is everything a matter of change and flux, of feelings and shifting opinions?" "Can truth be determined by a vote or by a show of hands?" Indeed, our world increasingly asks, much as a hand-washing Roman governor once asked Truth to His face, "What is truth?" (John 18:38).

Let us turn now to this great hound of the Lord who chased away countless threatening errors and hunted down an amazing bounty of truths that we so desperately need to reclaim as we examine the thinking of this tireless thinker, the doing of this indomitable doer, and the fervent loving acts of this most learned lover.

Albertus Magnus: Thinker

Born sometime between 1193 and 1206, Albert of Lauingen[83] lived through fourth-fifths of what has been called "the greatest of centuries"[84] and bore the title of *Magnus* (the Great) while he was still alive. This accolade was due to his incredible breadth of knowledge and mastery of virtually every scientific discipline known to man at the time—literally from A to Z, with contributions to fields as diverse as anatomy, anthropology, astronomy, biology, botany, chemistry, dentistry, geography, geology,

---

[83] This is what Albert called himself, suggesting his birth in the town of Lauingen, now in Bavaria.

[84] James J. Walsh, M.D., Ph.D., LL.D., Litt.D, Sc.D, *The Thirteenth: Greatest of Centuries* (New York: Catholic Summer School Press, 1920).

medicine, physiology, physics, psychology, and zoology. Some said that Albert knew all that there was to know! Indeed, Albert's knowledge as a scientist was matched by his knowledge of philosophy and theology too. He became the world's foremost academic professor and a hound of the Lord all the while.

So how did Great Albert get to be so great? To examine Saint Albert the thinker, we should start with young Albert the student. Albert's parents were of the lower nobility and apparently died when he and his siblings were relatively young. Albert was raised by his uncle. Although we don't have much detail on his early education, formal education was fairly rare at the time, a blessing reserved to the relatively well off and provided by teachers at the local cathedral or monastery. He would have likely received the lasting benefits of a medieval system of education based on the seven classical liberal arts. These consisted in the first years of the *trivium* (from *tri*, "three," and *via*, "roads") of grammar, dialectics or logic, and rhetoric, and later, of the *quadrivium* (four roads) of music theory, astronomy, geometry, and mathematics. Greek and Roman educators believed the *trivium* provided the fundamental tools for thinking that prepared one for adult life and that set the stage for all future specialized knowledge.[85] Medieval educators agreed (and perhaps we would be better off if more modern ones did too!).

---

[85] For a more detailed look at Albert's probable training, see my *Saint Albert the Great: Champion of Reason*, 16–20. For a masterful modern look at value of the *trivium*, see Dorothy Sayers's 1947 essay *The Lost Tools of Learning*, and for a comprehensive modern educational how-to book, see Sister Miriam Joseph's *The Trivium: The Liberal Arts of Logic, Grammar, and Rhetoric*, reissue edition (Philadelphia, PA: Paul Dry Books, 2002), originally published in 1948.

By learning the nature of inflected Latin, Albert grew to understand the fundamental nature of all languages. By learning logic, he discovered how to differentiate valid from invalid arguments and truths from falsehoods, so essential to Scholastic methods of higher education. By learning rhetoric, he saw the importance of carefully defining terms, the importance of a powerful memory, and the necessity of and methods for tailoring one's preaching or teaching to one's audience. We can see that the *trivium* was anything but trivial to Albert, since as a young man he chose to hone these tools of learning further by pursuing advanced education in the *trivium* and *quadrivium* at the University of Padua, the world's foremost center of learning of the liberal arts.

Albert's interest in learning was by no means limited to the formal classroom either. He was constantly enthralled by the creation all around him, showing great interest in plants, in animals of all sorts, including the fish in the Danube, in the terrain of the earth, and in the motion of the heavens. Indeed, it has been said that one could repopulate the forests of Bavaria with the plants and animals that would be described in Albert's books.

Struggling student? Some interesting legends surround Albert's early academic career as a student. One suggests that young Albert was not exactly a whiz kid, perhaps providing hope for those with high hopes and average intelligence! The story holds that early on at Padua, Albert had a hard time learning science. Everything that he had learned in the evening seemed to vanish from his mind by the time he woke up the next morning. Then one day his room shone brightly as Saints Catherine and Barbara and the Holy Virgin Mary suddenly appeared before him. The Blessed Mother asked him what he desired, and Albert responded by asking her for vast knowledge of human wisdom. The Holy Virgin responded that she would give him philosophical learning without equal. Further, addressing a common concern of the day, she told Albert that his human knowledge would never draw him away from the Faith.[86] Finally, she told him that before the end of his life on earth, his knowledge would leave him and he would return to God as simple and innocent as a child.

The biographer Joachim Sighart speculates that stories about Albert's difficulties in learning may have arisen because he spent so long in his studies. Saint Dominic, for example, with less interest in scientific knowledge, studied philosophy for six years, while Saint Albert's philosophical studies may have lasted as long as ten years. Further, Saint Albert himself had written that he always felt inspired to study by the Virgin Mary and what he could not master through study came to him through prayer.

Talented teacher. Nonetheless, by the time young Albert's studies were over, the stories of Albert the struggling student were replaced by stories of Albert as the most talented teacher of all. Saint Thomas Aquinas, commenting on Aristotle, wrote that "a characteristic of one possessing Science is his ability to

---

[86] Later in his life, while Dominican provincial of Germany, Albert himself would speak out in strong words against those opposed to acquiring human knowledge, the fideists of his day, even within the order: "There are those ignorant people who wish to combat by every means possible the use of philosophy, and especially among the preachers, where no one opposes them; senseless animals who blaspheme that of which they know nothing." Cited in Sister M. Albert's *Albert the Great* (Oxford: Blackfriars Publications, 1948), 39.

teach,"[87] and Albert taught like few before him or since. When his philosophical and theological training were complete around 1233, Albert attained the title of *lector* (reader) of theology at the Dominican convent of Cologne, Germany, about three hundred miles east of Paris. Seven years later, after organizing Dominican convent schools in Hildeshiem and Freiburg as well, he would be sent back those three hundred miles west to the home base of Dominican education and indeed the greatest center of learning in the world, the University of Paris, where he would ascend from *lector* to *doctor,* having attained the highest and foremost of academic degrees in 1244. That same year, the world's most talented teacher met the world's most studious student, when our next chapter's subject joined Saint Albert in Paris.

In 1248 Albert was appointed regent at a new Studium Generale back in Cologne. Our learned hounds of the Lord had multiplied so rapidly that the order's only center of higher studies at the Convent of Saint James in Paris could hardly kennel and train all four hundred to five hundred of them! One of the goals of the order's general chapter meeting in Paris that year was to establish additional houses of higher study in several Dominican provinces at Bologna for Italy, Montpellier for Provence, Oxford for England, and Cologne for Germany. Who better to establish the Dominican mini university of Cologne than Great Albert of Cologne himself? (And who better to accompany him as his aid than the young Thomas Aquinas?) There at Cologne, Albert's genius, as well as his sanctity, and the "force of his doctrine" drew students and scholars from around the world. It is no surprise, then, that two years later we find Albert at Vincennes in

---

[87] Saint Thomas Aquinas, *Commentary on Aristotle's Nichomachean Ethics* (Notre Dame, IN: Dumb Ox Books, 1994), 366.

northern France, helping draft the official system of study for the Order of Preachers.

Profound philosopher. As a teacher, Albert deftly passed on to his students the fruits of his contemplation, and his formalized scientific and philosophical contemplation of the works of creation continued well into his eighth decade. Albert not only studied and passed on what great thinkers had unearthed; he unearthed a good deal of new knowledge of his own. He introduced the brilliant works of Aristotle to the West in his meticulous, line-by-line commentaries on many of Aristotle's works, works that some feared threatened the Faith, since Aristotle reasoned, for example, that the universe was eternal and that God did not take interest in human affairs. Albert faithfully reported what Aristotle truly taught, the bulk of it being magnificent and in harmony with the truths of the Church. In his own later works, Albert was anything but a parrot of Aristotle's opinions in science and philosophy, however, contradicting him at times in specific matters (e.g., the frequency of lunar rainbows, the number of human ribs, and the dietary preferences of eels!) through his own experience or experimentation. Indeed, Albert even wrote a treatise on Aristotle's errors.

In the fields of science, or "natural philosophy," Albert was without peer in his day in his research and prolific writing; he wrote entire books on animals, vegetables, and minerals, for a few examples. His knowledge of chemistry and mineralogy sprouted myths that Albert was a great magician. Indeed, books about Albertus Magnus as magician (perhaps in part confusing *magnus*, "great," with *magus*, "magician") are still on the market today!

Memory master. Albert probed deeply into the realm of philosophical psychology as well, wresting deep secrets of the nature of the human soul in its passions or emotions, intellect, and will. To highlight in brief an area of special interest to me, Albert played a pivotal role in the history of mnemonics, or memory improvement techniques. An ancient work on the "method of loci," a system of memory improvement using graphic mental visual images and a series of imagined locations as an ordering technique was attributed to the poet Simonides (sixth century B.C.) and had been passed on from ancient Greece and Rome in the surviving writings of Marcus Tullius Cicero (first century B.C.). A separate ancient work on the nature of the workings of human memory had come down through the writings of Aristotle. Saint Albert went over them both with the fine-toothed comb of his intellect and successfully merged these two ancient streams of knowledge on memory *improvement* and on *the nature of* memory, providing a rushing river of insights into both. Further, while the memory improvement methods were historically used primarily as effective aids to *public speaking* (not by memorizing speeches word for word, but for keeping one's key points, the outline of one's talk more or less, in one's mind in its exact order), Saint Albert moved them as well into the realm of *ethical behavior*.

In Albert's great moral treatise *De Bono* (*On the Good*), when writing about the parts or components of the virtue of *prudence*, or practical wisdom, Albert borrowed Cicero's three parts of *memory, understanding,* and *foresight,* for to achieve ethical goals in the future, we must act on our present understanding, based on what we have learned in the past. Indeed, Albert would consider memory the most important part of the virtue of prudence, and he would, in no uncertain terms, recommend formal memory training as an ethical endeavor:

> Whence we say that among all those things which point
> towards ethical wisdom, the most necessary is trained

memory, because from past events we are guided in the present and the future, and not from the converse.[88]

And as for the particular "method of loci" endorsed by Cicero (Tully), Albert would make clear:

> We say that art of memory is best which Tully teaches, above all with respect to those things-for-remembering which pertain to how we live and to justice, and these memories chiefly relate to ethics, it is necessary that this art be within the soul through corporeal images; in these images however it will not remain except within the memory.[89]

Albert was one of history's greatest thinkers. We have provided but the smallest of nutshells here, although the mighty oak of his encyclopedic knowledge can't help but be seen in how it branched out far and wide into his activities as a doer and a thinker.

Albertus Magnus: Doer

Now we move from Albert the thinker, to Albert the *doer*, from the one who contemplates to the one who passes on the fruits of his contemplation. We'll quickly survey this great thinker's

---

[88] From *De Bono*, cited in Mary Carruthers, *The Book of Memory: A Study of Memory in Medieval Culture* (Cambridge: Cambridge University Press, 1990), 275.

[89] Ibid. For detailed expositions and how-to tutorials on these methods, see my previous books *Memorize the Faith! (And Most Anything Else) Using the Methods of the Great Catholic Medieval Memory Masters* (Sophia Institute Press, 2006) and *Memorize the Reasons! Defending the Faith with the Catholic Art of Memory* (Catholic Answers Press, 2013).

doings in several important and official roles—as a son of Saint Dominic, a preacher of the Word, a leader of a province, a bishop of a diocese, a crusader for Christendom, and a peacemaker in service of the pope.

Docile Dominican. It seems most fitting indeed for young Albert to have been drawn to the vibrant new order of hounds of the Lord, so focused on learning and sharing Christ's good news, as Albert was so enamored of both. He frequented the Dominican Church in Padua and was drawn to the order despite the protests of his uncle, who had hoped he would become a government official. A fascinating story is told about Albert's decision to enter the order, having been enthralled by the powerful and joyous preaching of Jordan of Saxony, Saint Dominic's successor as master general of the order.[90] It was said that young Albert had a dream in which he entered the order but left it soon after. He awoke feeling blessed by this forewarning of a grave mistake in the discernment of his vocation. Later that day, however, he attended a sermon in which Master Jordan declared that the devil sometimes subtly deceives men by telling them in their dreams that they will enter the order but not persevere! Albert sought out Master Jordan and asked how he had read his heart. Jordan comforted and encouraged him, and sometime around 1233, Albert entered the Order of Preachers, much to the devil's consternation.

Prudent preacher. Even before he attained fame as a talented teacher, Albert became a most prudent preacher. Although his knowledge was vast and deep and grew every day, Albert did

---

[90] We took a brief look at the life of Blessed Jordan with More Hounds of the Lord following chapter 1.

not talk over the heads of medieval congregations. He was not known as a particularly powerful or flamboyant preacher, and his homilies did not draw people from all over the world, as his lectures always did, yet he was an effective preacher who could touch the hearts of his listeners and inspire them to good acts in their daily lives. He abounded in earthy examples and in homespun wit. Indeed, it was during a sermon on Luke 16:19–31, on the story of poor Lazarus and Dives the rich man, particularly 16:21, "the dogs came and licked his sores," that Albert preached the phrase that set the theme for this book: "The roving dogs are the Order of Preachers who do not wait at their homes for the poor but go out to them and lick the ulcers of their sins, having in their mouths the bark of preaching." Albert's homilies were brief and consisted of three main parts: (1) a short and straightforward *literal explanation* of a scriptural passage, (2) an *allegorical and mystical interpretation* of the passage, and (3) a *summary* of the message in clear-cut language, often cast in the form of a *prayer* that God would grant the congregation the spiritual fruits that should accrue from pondering and applying his sacred lessons.

Providential provincial. In 1254, while praying at Saint Peter's in Rome, a religious received a vision that a massive serpent had writhed into the basilica with horrible hissing that was heard throughout Rome. Then a man came forth in the habit of the Order of Preachers, and his name was given as Albert. The serpent attacked the Dominican, but he broke free and ascended the pulpit, whereupon he read from the Gospel of Saint John up to the words "Verbum caro factum est et habitavit in nobis" ("And the Word became flesh and dwelt among us"; 1:14), and at these words, the serpent fled and ceased its hissing. When Albert did in fact arrive in Rome later that year, the man told him of his vision, but Albert could not discern its meaning.

Also in 1254, at the ancient city of Worms, the same Albert had served the order so well as a teacher and preacher that he was elected the provincial of the German Province, a massive jurisdiction with more than forty convents and extending as far north as the English Sea, as far east as Poland, and as far south and west as the whole of Austria and Switzerland. Albert served as a firm but loving leader, traveling countless miles by foot to visit and improve the spiritual welfare of dozens of convents of men and women. He established three new convents for men and one for women. Ever the preacher, Albert sought to help perfect the Dominicans in their primary call to preaching by decreeing that no one could preach outside his convent walls until he had done so frequently within them. Ever the saintly scientist, Albert would stop first at each priory's chapel for prayer and in the evening would visit its library, where he would drink in the wealth of rare manuscripts. Indeed, cited in some of Albert's own books are medieval literary treasures that have been lost to us and have not been cited since. He also left writings of his own at some of the fortunate priories. As Saint Paul left behind him in his travels a trail of his own handmade tents, Saint Albert left behind at many of these priories a trail of his own handmade texts.

In 1256 Albert had been called to the papal court of Pope Alexander at Anagni to defend the mendicant orders of the Dominicans and the Franciscans at the University of Paris. Certain secular teachers had been spreading tales about the friars there. Albert mounted a successful defense, and the pope was so impressed with Albert's eloquence and knowledge that he retained him to preach the gospel to the papal court from the

Gospel of Saint John — "Verbum caro factum est et habitavit in nobis" and more!

Booted bishop. After three years or so, Albert resigned as provincial because he yearned to return to his life of learning and teaching. After but four years of respite, a call would come from Rome concerning Albert that would alter the course of his life and would shake to the core the soul of his order's master general — chapter 2's Blessed Humbert of Romans. The important German diocese of Ratisbon (aka Regensburg) stood in a state of near financial, political, and spiritual ruin. Pope Alexander IV had been so impressed with Albert's lectures to the papal curia and with his deft administration as a provincial that he chose him for the office of bishop. Although many Dominicans had become bishops (indeed, thirty had attended the Council of Lyons fifteen years before), the thought of Great Albert as bishop cut Blessed Humbert to the core. He wrote that it would be a terrible scandal for Albert to take the episcopacy and indeed that he would rather hear of Albert's lying in a grave than sitting upon a bishop's throne!

Major bishoprics in those days came with great earthly wealth and political powers. The clerical equivalent of secular princes, some bishops even had their own armies. It seems that Blessed Humbert's concerns were much more for the possible bad impression this could make on other Dominicans than for any real peril to Albert's soul. Perhaps he even hoped that Albert would succeed him one day as Dominican master general. Eventually though, Albert obeyed the will of Saint Peter's successor and became the Bishop of Ratisbon.

Although he served for only a couple of years, Albert's knowledge of science in the broadest sense of the study of causes and effects, and perhaps his knowledge of agriculture too, enabled him to examine the physical needs of the diocese, put all episcopal properties under full cultivation, and greatly increase the diocese's income. Never forgetting Saint Dominic's call to poverty, he also reined in reckless spending, sold off unneeded luxuries, and gave unneeded furniture from the episcopal palace to the poor, digging the diocese out from under the debt he had inherited of 486 pounds of gold. Never forgetting the personal call to poverty either, his bishop's dress was fitting for the title, but not excessive, with a modest miter. The most notable feature of his attire was the retention of the crude footwear he wore as a Dominican when he traveled from town to town, earning him the nickname of *episcopus com botis* — Bishop Boots!

Albert was also an able administrator in many other ways, always strengthening the houses of religious orders, reminding the clergy of their spiritual duties, changing the feast day of the dedication of a Benedictine monastery to a Sunday so pilgrims would not lose a day's wages, organizing the fundraising for a hospice, and working together with four other bishops so that people who had committed crimes against the Church could not find safe haven in a neighboring diocese.

Coped crusader.[91] Albert had proved himself a most able doer and shepherd to his flock, but he yearned to return to a life of contemplation and teaching and resigned his bishopric in 1262. Hardly a year had gone by, though, when Albert again received a papal call, this time to preach a crusade. Several years before,

---

[91] A cope (or cape) is a long liturgical garment that is open in front and held together by an ornamental clasp. Albert wore one as a bishop. As a Dominican friar, Albert wore the coarse white woolen habit of his order.

in 1256, some sources report that Albert and a small group of peers had been sent to the frontier lands of Poland, Prussia, and Livonia in the office of a papal legate. There he was horrified to find a barbaric society that we might well call a "culture of death" in lands once converted by Saints Hyacinth and his brother Ceslaus.[92] And what were their horrible crimes? They slaughtered children born with deformities, artificially limited the size of their families, and euthanized the elderly who had become a burden. Indeed, they would proudly point out the grave of their own parents they had slaughtered. Albert was outraged that they still dared to call themselves Christians. (How eerily similar are their practices to some today who also claim the Christian name.)

We don't have extensive documentation of that mission, but some report that it had some success and was part of the reason Pope Urban IV, former patriarch of Jerusalem, would call upon Albert to preach the eighth crusade, recruiting warriors and resources throughout Germany. Albert signed his last letter as *Praedicator Crucis*, Preacher of the Cross for the Crusade, on August 25, 1264. Less than six weeks later, Pope Urban IV passed away, and the eighth crusade would not commence for six years.

Pontifical peacemaker. Even more effective than as a preacher of war was Albert as a preacher of peace. Because of his vast knowledge, impeccable judgment, and personal virtue, Albert was often called in throughout the years of his adult life to settle disputes between various clerical, religious, and secular parties. In perhaps his most dramatic series of negotiations from the early 1250s to 1260, Albert negotiated between the powerful and warlike Conrad, Archbishop of Hochstaden, "next to the Emperor

---

[92] As we saw in More Hounds of the Lord: Saint Hyacinth of Poland.

... the most powerful and the first Prince of the State,"[93] and the merchants and townspeople of his diocese. The first encounter came about after Conrad levied a heavy tax on merchants and established a customs house in Neuss, a small town across the Rhine from Cologne. The citizens responded by smuggling goods to avoid the tolls. He also minted his own money, prompting municipal leaders to seek him out at his palace to voice their complaints. Conrad responded by sailing warships down the Rhine to battle the citizenry of Cologne. He was sorely vexed that the citizens refused to be drawn out in battle but had settled in for a siege. At the prompting of an overly optimistic military engineer, he sent a boat loaded with "Greek fire"—a deadly mixture of combustible fluids—down the Rhine to destroy a merchant fleet, but that boat itself was the only vessel that went up in smoke.[94] Albert was called to the negotiating rescue and brokered a peace that would last a few years. In fact, he would broker the peace three times before the contentious archbishop would meet his maker in the year 1260.

Albert was a consummate peacemaker because he knew well that peace is a concordance of harmony or desires among persons. When those persons' desires are not fully just and their thoughts are not focused on good and honorable ends, peace will not last long. This played out in the transient effects of some of Albert's wise arbitrations. He knew that true peace was possible only among good men, and that is why his greatest peacemaking efforts were performed not in the settlement of sundry disputes

---

[93] Joachim Sighart, *Albert the Great: His Life and Scholastic Labours: From Original Documents* (Charleston, SC: Bibilolife, 2009), 168.

[94] Can you imagine your bishop sailing a fleet of warships down your local river to besiege your city? (I hope not!)

over worldly goods, but through his teaching and preaching the gospel of Christ *in order to make men good.*

Albertus Magnus: Lover

Mary's minstrel. Although a man of unmatched scientific knowledge and formidable administrative know-how to boot, Albert the great thinker and doer was equaled by Albert the great lover. The dearest object of his love, after the Creator, of course, was the sweetest of the Creator's creations. We have seen the legends of how Mary inspired him to study and won for him from God the ability to gain vast knowledge. In quieter times toward the end of his life, Albert would compose and sing hymns to her as he prayed in the cloister garden. Although there is some question of the attribution to Albert of some of his writings, such as the fascinating *Mariale* or *230 Questions concerning the Virgin,*[95] Albert may have written more about the Blessed Mother than any theologian of his era.

As to a sample of his Mary-inspired eloquence, King Solomon asks, "Who is this that looks forth like the dawn, fair as the moon, bright as the sun?" (Song of Sol. 6:10). Albert answers that the dawn is Mary. The night is her eternal predestination, and she is the dawn that ushers in the full and perfect light of the Son. She is "the dawn of all grace unto our glory — the dawn rising in the fullness of grace and yet growing even into the perfection of day."[96]

[95] Considered by some to be among the earliest of his works, it addresses a full ninety questions to Mary's virtues and graces and does not hesitate to consider such details as her height, the cast of her complexion, and the color of her hair and eyes!

[96] From Rev. Robert J. Bushmiller, *The Maternity of Mary in the Mariology of Saint Albert the Great,* dissertation (University of

Central to Albert's Mariology is Mary's divine maternity, her predestined honor to be the bearer of God incarnate, for an even higher grace than being the son of God by adoption is to be the Mother of God by nature. Indeed, ever the Aristotelian philosopher, he notes that to be "the Mother of God by nature though not God" is a mean between "being the Son of God by nature and truly God, and being the Son of God by adoption and not God."

Albert's love of Mary was recognized closer to our time, when on November 1, 1950, nearly seven hundred years after Albert's death, Pope Pius XII, in defining the dogma of the Assumption of Mary, wrote:

> When, during the Middle Ages, scholastic theology was especially flourishing, St Albert the Great, who to establish this teaching had gathered together many proofs from Sacred Scripture, from the statements of older writers, and finally from the liturgy and from what is known as theological reasoning, concluded in this way: "From these proofs and authorities and from many others, it is manifest that the most blessed Mother of God has been assumed above the choirs of angels." And this we believe in every way to be true.[97]

Lady lover. Dominican tradition holds that when the first Dominican friars reached Germany in the early thirteenth century, they

---

Fribourg, Switzerland, 1959), 27, citing from Albert's *De Naturi Boni* (*On the Nature of the Good*).

[97] Pope Pius XII, apostolic constitution defining the dogma of the Assumption, November 1, 1950, cited in Cheryl Dickow, *Mary, Ever Virgin, Full of Grace: A Study of Papal Encyclicals on Mary* (Waterford, MI: Bezalel Books, 2010), 89.

already found there groups of holy women, some of them living in poverty and even wearing religious habits. By the time of Saint Albert's death in the last quarter of that century, the German province would be blessed with sixty-five convents, more than in the rest of the provinces combined. Albert was very attentive to the holy women of the order who lived lives of contemplative prayer, and he was loved as preacher and confessor. Many stories survive about Albert and the holy Dominican nuns, and I'll highlight a few of them, in brief.

The first incident occurred around 1237 and prefigures an event in the life of young Saint Thomas that we'll address in our next chapter. One Iolanda, daughter of Count Vianden and great-niece of the Byzantine Emperor, took a religious habit at the convent of Marienthal. Sore vexed by this eighteen-year-old's swift decision, her family stormed the convent and brought her back home to the family castle, and whom did they call in to talk sense to her but the wise young professor already known for his unsurpassed wisdom and justice. Albert discerned her true zeal and convinced her parents to let her return to the convent. Not only did she do so, but later, after her father had died in a crusade, her mother joined her as a religious at Marienthal, and her brother become a Dominican friar.

Albert also played a key role in the founding of a great convent that would become known as Paradise. In 1252, the order's fourth master general, John of Wildhausen, conceived the idea of a great convent in the diocese of Cologne. The friars proceeded to preach and solicit to build this holy haven, and donations came in aplenty—not only in money and in property, but even in lives. Wealthy and prominent citizens sought admittance for their wives and daughters. In 1259, the bishop of Osnabruck called in none other than Albert, then the German provincial, to instruct this group of holy women in the Rule of Saint Augustine and the constitutions of the Order of Preachers. After the women's formal profession, the convent's first prior declared that the convent would be known as Paradise, a joyous earthly prelude to heaven.

Other stories are said to have occurred after Albert was in the true heavenly paradise. A fifteenth-century biographer, Peter of Prussia, cites an apparition to Saint Mechtilde of Helfta in the 1290s that appeared in the *Little Treatise on Spiritual Graces* that Henry of Halle had put together from the saint's *Revelations*. She reported a vision of two great saints approaching the throne of "the King of the mansion of the saints." Escorted by angels, the two saints wore beautiful garments with bright letters of gold that represented the knowledge of Christ's divinity and humanity that they taught in their books. They had become "like saints" because "they sought during their passing life to resemble them in everything by their virtues and knowledge." They would indeed be officially canonized as saints one day, the first in 1323, and the second in 1931. They were Saint Thomas Aquinas and his beloved mentor, Saint Albert the Great.

Thorough theologian. Albert's greatest love of all, of course, was his love for God.

Albert so loved the natural sciences, waxing eloquent in his writings on everything from flowers to insects to fish to the squirrelly daily habits of the squirrels, because they all in small, diverse ways reflected the unspeakable, simple goodness and majesty of the Creator, from whom all creation flows. Albert knew so well how God speaks to us through creation, but he also knew that God has spoken to us directly too, in His revelation, and most directly of all through the words and the deeds of His Son incarnate.

Albert's love for God is seen in his extensive knowledge of the Scriptures, of Church history, of the liturgy, and of the Eucharist. Albert left extensive commentaries on the Scriptures, among the most prominent being his *Commentary on Saint Luke's Gospel.* He wrote beautifully about the Eucharist and offered practical advice on mastering the art of prayer to express our love for God.

Perhaps Albert's most significant purely spiritual work, *De Adherendo Deo* (*On Cleaving to God*), is one that he might have not written in its entirety.[98] The beautifully simple, although profoundly moving book, which has been called a worthy companion to Thomas à Kempis's *Imitation of Christ*, is about "cleaving freely, confidently, nakedly, and firmly to God alone ... since the goal of Christian perfection is the love by which we cleave to God."

Charging champion. The virtue of *fortitude* comes from the Latin *fortis*, "strength." Saints Albert and Thomas would write a great deal about the nature of virtues, including fortitude, and Albert clearly not only *knew* of this spiritual strength but did not shy away from *living* it. Fortitude employs the irascible appetite and

---

[98] It has long been attributed to Saint Albert, but modern scholars point to references that suggest that it was penned not in the thirteenth century but the fifteenth. Still others note that of the book's seventeen chapters, the first nine hang together in a way that the last seven do not, suggesting perhaps that Albert wrote those chapters and the others were later accretions. Whatever the truth might be, the book abounds in sources and concepts dear to Albert, including Aristotle's theory of the intellect, Saint Augustine's parts of the human soul (reason, memory, and will), mirroring the Trinity, and the neo-Platonic philosopher Dionysius (or "pseudo-Dionysius" to distinguish him from Dionysius the Aeropagite, converted by Saint Paul as described in Acts 17:34).

can raise our ire to fight back to defend the good, even when this means facing difficult obstacles. We saw that Albert was happy bravely to champion the cause of the rights of the Dominicans and Franciscans when challenged by the secular professors of the University of Paris. We saw too a flicker of Albertian ire when he railed at those even within his order who tried to squelch the study of philosophy. Perhaps the most poignant and powerful example of Albertian fortitude, though, is how he defended his own greatest student not long after that student's death.

On March 7, 1277, three years to the day after the death of Thomas Aquinas, Bishop Steven Tempier of Paris, having solicited input from various theologians, produced 218 propositions that were said to be contrary to the Catholic Faith. Among that list, sixteen propositions were clearly compatible with the writings of Thomas Aquinas.[99] Some reports indicate that the elderly Albert traveled the three hundred miles to Paris on foot to meet Tempier's challenge and champion his brilliant student's thought. He began his speech to the learned professors by stating, "What glory it is for one who is living to be praised by

---

[99] These concerned some very abstruse and technical philosophical and theological issues. One example is that the bishop's list condemned the idea that "the vegetative, sensitive, and intellective [souls] constitute one simple form." Saint Augustine and others had taught that the matter can be "informed" by multiple forms, that we possess vegetative, sensitive, and intellectual souls, and that the body possessed a form of its own before the other forms. Thomas, following Aristotle, taught the "unicity" or the "oneness" of the human soul, that we are not two natures (body and spirit) put together, but that the union of body and spirit is what makes our single human nature. Further, humans have but *one soul* that possesses vegetative (development, growth, reproduction), sensitive (sensation and movement) and intellectual (reasoning) *powers*.

those who are dead." He went on to portray Saint Thomas as the one who truly lived, while his accusers of unorthodoxy were covered in shades of death through their ignorance and ill will. He defended the orthodoxy of Thomas's writings, along with Thomas's personal sanctity, offering to defend them both before an assemblage of competent men. He returned to Cologne and poured over Thomas's writings, declaring to an assemblage of Dominicans that Thomas's works were so masterful that he had "labored for all to the end of the world, and that henceforth all others would work in vain."[100]

Of course, the writings of Saint Thomas did not put an end to works in theology but would stimulate an endless stream of new work inspired by his brilliance as the Dominican Order and countless popes across the centuries have sung the praises for his works of theology. Thomas's philosophical and theological sons and daughters would come to be called Thomists, and Albert himself is the first and the foremost among them.

Cherished child. For many decades Albert the Great shone as one of the brightest lights in one of the greatest of centuries. His learning was unequalled, and he was known far and wide as a man who could get things done. The bark of his preaching and teaching had inflamed the hearts of countless students, friars, nuns, and parishioners who had heard and seen him. Recall, though, the legend that Blessed Mary had foretold that at the end of his days he would be bereft of his vast knowledge. A poignant tale records that Archbishop Sigfried had come to the Dominican convent to visit the elderly Albert one day and, knocking at the door of his cell, called out, "Albert, are you there?" The venerable master did not open the door, but merely

---

[100] Sighart, *Albert the Great*, 370.

answered: "Albert is no longer here; he was here once upon a time."[101]

It is said that the greatest encyclopedic mind of the century, the medieval memory master, began to lose his memory in the last weeks of his life. He retained the ability to say Mass, as he had done for so many years, but he removed himself ever more from the world, content to pray in his garden and his cell. The boots that had taken him all across Europe carried him daily to the site he had selected as the resting place of his body, as he prayerfully and peacefully prepared for the inevitable day of his death. His spirit strove solely to cleave closer to God.

In the twilight hours of November 15, 1280, clothed in the habit of the Order of Preachers, seated in a large wooden chair in his cell and surrounded by his brother friars in Christ, Saint Albert whispered that it had been a good thing to be a Dominican, and then, like a cherished child, his soul left to meet his heavenly Father and Mother.

Many centuries would pass as the process unfolded through which he who was acknowledged as "the Great" while he lived would be acknowledged as "the saint" in our time. Albert was canonized and declared a Doctor of the Church (*Doctor Universalis*, the "Universal Doctor") by Pope Pius XI on December 16, 1931. Ten years later to the day, Pope Pius XII (himself a Third Order Dominican) declared Saint Albert the patron saint of scientists. The 1930s and 1940s were a time like ours that cried out for this saintly scientist. Hear the eloquent words of a Dominican of that time:

> The modern scientist has introduced the world to the most complete power of devastation so far known — the

---

[101] Sighart, *Albert the Great*, 416.

atom bomb. The medieval scientist, Albert the Great, introduced the world to the most complete human power of synthesis so far realized—Saint Thomas Aquinas. The atom bomb is the result of the materialism and atheism of modern scientists. The *Summa Theologica* was the outcome of the wisdom and piety of the saintly Master of Cologne.[102]

It is time now to move from the saintly master to the most masterful and saintly student that a hound of the Lord has ever unleashed on the world.

---

[102] Conrad Pepler, O.P., preface to Sister M. Albert, O.P., *Albert the Great*, ix.

Saint Vincent Ferrer

1350–1419 | FEAST: APRIL 5

Saint Vincent Ferrer patterned his life after Saint Dominic's, and reports indicate the two even looked a lot alike — medium height, fair skin and hair, large, beautiful eyes, and an angelic demeanor. A gifted young scholar, Saint Vincent Ferrer would come to be known as "Thaumaturgus," or "Wonder Worker," as well as a zealous apostle for Christ, preaching and converting souls from Spain to Switzerland, from Italy to Scotland, and in most of Europe in between. Indeed, he virtually learned the Scriptures by heart and used that knowledge to convert thousands of Muslims and heretics. He also converted many thousands of Jews, and under his influence, the Jews of Valencia, Spain, converted their synagogue into a church.

Renowned for his passion and eloquence as a preacher, Saint Vincent usually prayed extensively to prepare for his sermons, but once, in preparation for a homily in which a very important nobleman would be in attendance, he studied extensively instead. The nobleman was not particularly impressed. Later, unbeknownst to Saint Vincent, he came to hear another homily and was deeply moved by the saint's message. When told this story, Saint Vincent replied that he had given the first homily, but Jesus Himself had given the second! This great Dominican thinker and doer wrote a simple and practical *Treatise on the Spiritual Life* in which he discussed, among many things, the

116

true nature of study: "Do you desire to study to your advantage? Let devotion accompany all your studies, and study less to make yourself learned than to become a saint." His studies and his prayers contributed to his own saintliness, and perhaps his example and his intercession will contribute to ours.

Saint Thomas Aquinas Shares God's Gift of Wisdom

Rigans montes de superioribus suis:
de fructu operum tuorum satiabitur terra.

From your heights you water the mountains;
the earth is filled with the fruits of your works.
—Psalm 103:13, Vulgate (RSVCE: Psalm 104:13)

The study of Saint Thomas is like climbing a mountain.
It is hard work but you are going up a path made by a towering
intellect. At the summit is wisdom. Should you attain it you
can stand tall and admire God and His greatness. Then
you can look down on human affairs and judge them.
—Carol Robinson, *My Life with Saint Thomas Aquinas*

Thomism is a form of wisdom.
—Raissa Maritain, *Saint Thomas Aquinas: Angel of the Schools*

God's Gift of Wisdom to the Hounds of the Lord

Wisdom, said Saint Thomas Aquinas, like Aristotle, is the
highest of the intellectual virtues of the mind, those God-given

natural capacities that enable man alone among all creatures on earth to seek and to find the truth. The virtue of *science* or *knowledge* provides us with the ability to acquire factual information to form conclusions about causes and effects operating in the things and events we observe in reality. The virtue of *understanding* allows us to delve deeper, to arrive at higher generalizations of those "Aha!" experiences by which we grasp underlying laws and principles that make sense of the particulars we observe. Highest of all, though, is the virtue of wisdom, as Saint Thomas explains:

> Science depends on understanding as on a virtue of higher degree: and both of these depend on wisdom, as obtaining the highest place, and containing beneath itself understanding and science, by judging both of the conclusions of science, and of the principles on which they are based.[103]

Wisdom looks at the biggest picture, rises to the greatest of heights, and focuses on the matters that matter the most. Saint Thomas's life was a life of wisdom, and perhaps his greatest gifts to us, the one-and-a-half-million-word *Summa Theologica*, has aptly been called one of the Holy Spirit's gifts of wisdom that we can hold in our hands!

Let's take a brief look at the life of this man who lived, breathed, and wrote wisdom, before we dig into the wisdom he gave us to grow leaps and bounds in our thinking, doing, and loving.

An Ox in a Nutshell

Thomas Aquinas lived from approximately 1225 to March 7, 1274. The privileged seventh child of an Italian lord and a

[103] *ST*, I-II, Q. 57, art. 2.

relative of the imperial family,[104] Thomas nonetheless sought the robe of a poor Dominican friar to live his life as a preacher and teacher. So dogged was he in the pursuit of truth that he would become among the most illustrious of all the hounds of the Lord and among the most illuminating of all theologians in the two-thousand-year history of Christendom.

Thomas bore the gift of a marvelously powerful intellect, exercised it to the full, and dedicated and directed it to the highest possible object: God. In early childhood his most burning, repeated question to all was "What is God?" He spent his whole life seeking the answer. As a young man, he would study under the incomparably learned Saint Albert the Great.[105] He would spend his mature adulthood as a teacher of theology, most notably at the University of Paris.

Saint Thomas lived his life humbly and gently, absorbed in the contemplation of God and in sharing with others the fruits of his contemplation. Even today we still savor them. Saint Thomas was perhaps the greatest integrator and synthesizer of truths in all of human history. He is the man who "baptized" Aristotle, the greatest of pagan philosophers, harnessing the truths Aristotle taught for the service of the Church. His knowledge

---

[104] Thank God Count Landulf of Aquino and Countess Theodora of Teano were so open to life. (And yet this family was not really so big, as we'll see when we come to the story of Saint Catherine of Siena!)

[105] In his youth, among his fellow students, because of his massive frame and his quiet demeanor, he acquired the nickname "the Dumb Ox." Albert the Great knew genius when he saw it and famously exclaimed to Thomas's classmates that "someday the bellowing of this ox will be heard around the world." (Thankfully, we can still hear the bellowing to this day, if we simply read Saint Thomas's works aloud!)

of and reverence for the Church Fathers was so great that Pope Leo XIII, citing Cardinal Cajetan, a Dominican master general, declared in his encyclical *Aeterni Patris* that Saint Thomas had "inherited the intellect of them all." But by far his greatest font of wisdom was God's divine revelation provided in the Scriptures. The *Summa Theologica* absolutely bristles with scriptural citations and insights on virtually every page.

Saint Thomas was canonized in 1323 and designated a Doctor of the Church in 1567. He is known as the Angelic Doctor because of his detailed writings on the angels (to which we'll devote a few minutes in these pages) and because of his most angelic demeanor. He is also known as the Common Doctor because his thought is of universal applicability to all Catholics across the centuries and across the world. (After all, truth is truth, regardless of time or locale!)

Let's move on, then, and examine the Angelic and Common Doctor through our lenses of thinking, doing, and loving (lenses that he helped to craft). So great is Saint Thomas's contribution to thought and thinking that we'll examine it in two sections: *how* he thought and *what* he thought about.

Saint Thomas Aquinas and the Art of Thinking

Saint Thomas's eventual unmatched mastery of the art of thinking was grounded in a spirit of the virtue of *humility* evident even in his infancy according to pious legends. As the stories go, years before this precocious five-year-old who was entrusted to the care of Benedictines of the Monastery of Monte Casino would ask the holy monks, "What is God?" he evidenced a wholly holy thirst for knowledge. One day when his mother, Theodora, took him to the baths of Naples, he grabbed a piece of paper and refused to let go of it, bawling when it was taken from him. His mother found that the Hail Mary was written on it and, in the interest of peace and quiet, she let him take it with him to the bath. His early biographer, William of Tocco, reported that, after that, the only sure way to keep young Thomas from crying was to give something written on a piece of paper.[106]

In these stories we see the very young Thomas thirsting for truth and realizing that to find it he first must seek it out, asking questions of others. Here is that nascent humility in its earliest form, and even in his full maturity, for the greatest of all intellects would never assume that he knew it all. Thomas, like Aristotle, whenever addressing any topic worth addressing, would examine what great minds before his had to say on the matter. This is intellectual humility, far from servility, and at the opposite pole from the intellectual hubris that has led so much of modern philosophy astray with philosophers who have acted as if philosophy began only when they reached the age of reason.

We saw that Pope Leo XIII, echoing the sixteenth-century Thomistic commentator Cardinal Cajetan, wrote that because Thomas so respected, venerated, and studied the thoughts of the great Church Fathers and Doctors who came before him, he seemed to have "inherited the intellect of all." So, from Thomas's humility came a respect for authority, for those who came before him and applied their great minds to great issues. Still, Thomas was a Dominican through and through, and one of their great mottos, as we have seen, is simply "Veritas!" or truth, and

---

[106] Simon Tugwell, O.P., has astutely observed, "His taste for books apparently antedated his ability to read!" Simon Tugwell, *Albert and Thomas: Selected Writings* (New York: Paulist Press, 1988), 202.

that is what Saint Thomas's intellect respected most of all. He loved truth wherever it was found and regardless of who said it. That is why he studied pagan, Jewish, and Arabic philosophers as well as Christian philosophers and theologians. He knew that God gave the great gift of reason to all men, and sometimes great truths may be found even within works with great errors as well. It is up to the seeker of truth to discern the wheat from the chaff, the true from the false. This applied as well to the Church Fathers he loved so much. He knew they possessed God's gift of reason, but that they, like him and all people, were not immune from error.[107]

Thomas, then, was not beyond questioning authority, except the authority of God and of the Church Christ established on earth. Indeed, he would write, "Although argument form authority based on human reason is the weakest, yet the argument from authority based on divine revelation is the strongest."[108]

Thomas so respected the capacities that God gave to man for thinking that he wrote about these powers extensively in his great *Summa Theologica* and particularly in his line-by-line analysis of Aristotle's understanding of human intellectual capacities in his

---

[107] Excepting, of course, the pope, in those special circumstances concerning faith and morals, wherein he stands incapable of error. As Thomas himself would write: "The Universal Church cannot err, since she is governed by the Holy Ghost, Who is the Spirit of Truth" (Saint Thomas Aquinas, *ST*, II-II, Q. 1, art. 90), and further, regarding the pope, to him belongs "authority which is empowered to decide matters of faith finally, so that they may be held by all with unshakeable faith. Now this belongs to the authority of the Sovereign Pontiff, to whom the more difficult questions that arise in the Church are referred" (ibid., art. 10).

[108] *ST*, II-II, Q. 1, art. 8.

commentary on *De Anima* (*On the Soul*).[109] Of course, he did not merely write about these powers, but he used them as few others ever have.

Thomas's great respect for the thoughts of others and even greater devotion to finding the truth wherever it might be found are revealed to the highest degree in the very manner in which he wrote the greatest of his works. For each of the hundreds of big, important philosophical and theological questions addressed in thousands of articles or focused essays within his *Summa Theologica*, or summary of theology, Thomas begins by citing several cogent arguments *against* what he considers the true answer, and here I must point out another essential Thomistic tenet. While many thinkers in the past and in our day glorify the *search* for the truth but never seem to *find* it, Thomas believed that truths indeed can be found, some accessible to careful reasoning and some acquired through our faith in God, who is Truth with a capital *T*.[110] Further, while many today believe truth is something

---

[109] For a deep and thorough presentation of Aristotle's and Saint Thomas's psychologies, see Fr. Robert Brennan, *Thomistic Psychology: A Philosophical Analysis of the Nature of Man* (Macmillan, 1941). For accessible, popular condensations I direct you to part I of my *Unearthing Your Ten Talents: A Thomistic Guide to Spiritual Growth through the Virtues and the Gifts* (Sophia Institute Press, 2009) and to chapters 2 and 3 of my *One-Minute Aquinas: The Doctor's Quick Answers to Fundamental Questions* (Sophia Institute Press, 2014).

[110] No one sums up these lofty thoughts better than the Angelic Doctor himself: "Truth is found in the intellect as it apprehends a thing as it is; and in things according as they have being conformable to an intellect. This is to the greatest degree found in God. For His being is not only conformed to His intellect, but is the very act of His intellect; and His act of understanding is the measure and cause of every other being and of every

that *we* construct, "defining," and "redefining" things according
to our wills, or indeed, our wishful fantasies, Thomas believed in
the "correspondence theory" of truth, that a belief about something is true when our thoughts about the thing correspond to
the thing's objective reality. Things have natures, and it is up to
us to inquire into and reason soundly about them.

So then, in every article of the *Summa Theologica*, Saint
Thomas begins by carefully and respectfully presenting positions
contrary to his, sometimes complete with quotations that apparently support them from Scripture or renowned Church Fathers.
So carefully does Thomas present these contrary arguments that
some have noted that he presents them more forcefully than his
opponents themselves have done! Next, though, after three or so
contrary arguments called objections, Thomas states, "*Sed contra*"
(on the contrary) and provides a paragraph or so in which he typically includes a quotation in support of his conclusion.[111] Next,
he states, "*Respondeo*" (I answer that) and proceeds to give his
own reasoned conclusions. Not finished yet, he replies to each
of the objections he presented at the start, typically revealing
how the objection presented an incomplete or misconstrued
interpretation of the scriptural, patristic, or philosophical passage
it was based on. Talk about thorough!

So this then, in brief, is how Thomas thought and how he
laid out his thought processes for all to see — to see not Thomas
but the truths to which he pointed. It is time to find out what

---

other intellect, and He Himself is His own existence and act
of understanding. Whence it follows not only that truth is in
Him, but that He is truth itself, and the sovereign and first
truth" (*ST*, I, Q. 16, art. 5).

[111] Pay close attention in our next section for the greatest authority
of all cited in the *Sed contra* to *ST*, I, Q. 2, art. 3.

kind of things that consummate Dominican thinker sought to consummate with his thoughts.

Saint Thomas's Thoughts on the Matters That Matter the Most

Recall Aristotle's statement that "it is better to know a little about sublime things than a lot about mean things." Thomas knew this and lived this like few others, for his thoughts always centered on the most sublime things, that is, the things of God. Here, in the briefest of summaries, I'll highlight the few key areas of focus in Saint Thomas's magnum opus, the *Summa Theologica*.

Thomas the boy kept asking, "What is God?" Thomas the man wrote in his masterful *Summa Contra Gentiles*, "To use the words of Hilary: 'I am aware that I owe this to God as the chief duty of my life, that my every word and sense may speak of him.'"[112] And speak of him he did! In the span of twenty years or so, Thomas wrote millions of words[113] explaining the answers he had found about God through the God-given gift of reason, and the God-given gift of revelation that transcends but does not contradict it.

Thomas was a thinker of the absolutely first rank, and he specifically sought out *wisdom* rather than mere accumulation of facts, because wisdom seeks out the highest causes that explain and illuminate the most. And the highest of all causes, the cause that *explains* all that is, and not only explains, but *creates*

---

[112] *Summa Contra Gentiles*, bk. 1, chap. 2, par. 2.

[113] The *Summa Contra Gentiles*, for example, exceeds 350,000 words, the *Summa Theologica* 1,500,000, and those are but two of his many, many works. (To put things into perspective, this book in your hands contains about 63,000.)

and *sustains* all existence, is God. Thomas's writings about God
are diffused throughout his works, but two of the most direct,
powerful, and comprehensive treatments are in his two great
Summas, the *Summa Contra Gentiles*, and the *Summa Theologica*,
and I'll focus our brief discussion on his treatment in the latter,
the greatest of all his works.

After making ten points on the nature of theology at the
beginning of the *Summa Theologica*,[114] Thomas addresses in the
second question one of the things he's most famous for, the five
proofs of God's existence. Although he covers some of the proofs
in much greater detail elsewhere, such as in the first book of the
Summa Contra Gentiles, the couple of pages he addresses to them
in the *Summa Theologica* have generated countless words of analysis and commentary in the seven centuries since he wrote them.

Thomas begins his demonstration of the proof of God's existence by reason alone, first by arguing that God's existence
is *not* self-evident to us. Some say that an awareness of God is
implanted in our hearts, but Thomas argued that it exists there
only in a confused way. It is one thing to know that *someone*
approaches, but another thing to know that it is, for example,
Peter. All people seek happiness, but not all realize that our
complete happiness (beatitude) lies only in God. Although some
vague awareness of God is implanted in our nature, we do not
know God with an automatic certainty. People do indeed deny
His existence. "The fool says in his heart, 'There is no God'"
(Ps. 53:1). Now, if we did by nature possess an understanding
of God's *essence*, what He is, then it would be self-evident to us
that God exists because, unlike any creature, God's *essence* and

---

[114] *ST*, I, Q. 1, art. 1 (summarized in chapter 21 of my *One-Minute
Aquinas*).

existence are one,[115] but God's essence is imperfectly known to us, and our imperfect knowledge is achieved through reasoned argument or through revelation.

Before providing the five proofs, Thomas also addresses those who believe that God's existence cannot be proved by reason alone.[116] Some argued that belief in God's existence is purely a matter of faith and can be held only through a faith in the truths of revelation. Thomas fired back to the contrary with the very words of Scripture: "Ever since the creation of the world his invisible nature, namely, his eternal power and deity, has been clearly perceived in the things that have been made" (Rom. 1:20). Saint Paul made clear that it is valid to reason a

---

[115] This is a marvelous and even humorous highlight of Thomas's presentation of proofs of God's existence in the *Summa Theologica*. He uses many deep and lengthy philosophical arguments to explain to some extent the meaning and implications of the fact that God's essence and existence are one. In the "On the contrary," section of his article on the proofs, Thomas cites as his authority four simple words—of God Himself—*Ego sum qui sum* (I AM WHO I AM; Exod. 3:14).

[116] Please bear in mind the importance of being able to show that reason alone can demonstrate God's existence, especially in our day, when so many people deny the truths of Christian revelation, giving no credence to the divine authorship of Scripture and the Christ-given authority of the Catholic Church. Reason employed in the service of faith can be the bridge by which those who claim to live their lives by reason alone may find themselves crossing over to the fullness of Christ's truth. Pope Leo XIII wrote as much in his encyclical *Aeterni Patris* in 1879, when many intellectuals were rejecting Christianity for science (and it proved true for me in 2004, when the writings of Saint Thomas drew me back to Christ and the Church after twenty-five years of atheism induced by modern philosophy so ignorant of Saint Thomas Aquinas!).

posteriori—that is, from things already known to us—to things not yet known. We can see and know the effects of God and then reason from them to demonstrate His existence as their cause—because if an effect exists, we know that its cause must have preceded it. From this kind of careful observation and reasoning, we cannot deduce the fullness of the Christian faith, but we can derive preambles, or starting points of faith, such as God's very existence and some basic facts about His attributes. These preambles can also be starting points in our discussions with others who deny God's existence.

As for the five proofs themselves, I have not the time or space to discuss them in great detail here,[117] but bear in mind that so powerful are these arguments that they demonstrate the necessity of God's existence, *even if* we grant the point to some philosophers that *the universe always existed*. Thomas knew from revelation that God *created* the universe, but he believed that reason alone could not decide the matter. Aristotle, for example, believed that the universe always existed, but he also believed that reason proved that God must exist to *sustain* it. So then, Saint Thomas goes on briefly to lay out five arguments based on things that are evident to our senses when we look at the world. By the observations that (1) things move or change, (2) there are effects and causes, (3) things exist for a time and then perish, (4) there are varying degrees of goodness or perfection in things, and (5) there is ordered or purposeful behavior in nature, Thomas shows that there must exist (1) a first or unmoved mover, (2) a first or uncaused cause, (3) a necessary being that cannot not exist, (4) a perfection of being from which lesser degrees

---

[117] See *ST*, I, Q. 1, art. 3 for the proofs and chapter 22 of *The One-Minute Aquinas* for my attempt at a terse explanation.

of goodness flow, and (5) a first and final cause that provides for the order and governance of the entire universe. Bearing in mind that he grants the concession for argument's sake that the universe always existed, you will see that his arguments are not dependent, as many modern critics suppose, merely on time and do not require a chronological regression. The great chains of causation, perfection, order, and purpose require a prime mover, a first efficient cause, a necessary being, an ultimate formal cause, and a final cause for their existence, not merely sometime in the past, but *at this very moment.* "We live and move and have our being"[118] right now at this minute through the grace, love, and power of an eternal God.

Thomas then moves on to a wonderful exposition of God's attributes, His *simplicity, perfection, infinity, immutability, unity, goodness, immensity,* and *eternity,* before moving beyond reason alone and grappling with the glorious, revealed mysteries of the Holy Trinity. He next moves on to a consideration of creation, of the universe of goodness that springs forth from the loving generosity of the Creator. As the twentieth-century French Thomistic philosopher Jacques Maritain stated so eloquently, "Saint Thomas cast his net upon the universe and carried off all things, transformed into the life of the mind, towards the beatific vision."[119] Thomas's writings on creation must be read to be appreciated. I'll provide just a highlight or two.

If God is one, why is there such diversity in His creation? Thomas answers, "He produced many and diverse creatures, that what was wanting to one in the representation of the divine

---

[118] Acts 17:28. Saint Paul cites this line from the ancient Grecian philosopher and poet Epimenides.

[119] Maritain, *Saint Thomas Aquinas*, 66.

goodness, which in God is simple and uniform, in creatures is manifold and divided; and hence the whole universe together participates in the divine goodness more perfectly, and represents it better than any single creature whatever."[120] (We might ask ourselves what part we have been playing to represent God's divine goodness to others.)

Is it possible that God created the universe but takes no active role in it now? Thomas argues the astounding fact that God *sustains* our existence at every moment, preventing all that He created from returning to nothingness. Thomas says, "Every creature may be compared to God, as the air is to the sun which enlightens it."[121] Without the sun, the air becomes instantly dark. God is generous, active, and loving all right. He is the immediate and direct cause of all creatures, having created them and preserving their existence "by continually pouring out existence to them."[122] Saint Thomas, in essence, reminds us that when God's love rains and reigns (and it always does), it pours!

In the second of the three parts of Thomas's *Summa Theologica*, he addresses creation, and most specifically man, in about 1,500 pages brimming over with philosophical, psychological, and theological insights. God has poured us out as part of His creation. We rejoice in our existence but seek to return to Him, the source of our existence and the fulfillment of our happiness. In the *Summa Theologica's* second part, Saint Thomas addresses human nature and how God's grace perfects it. He treats of the sins that direct us from the path toward God, but even more so of the kinds of virtues that perfect the powers of our God-given

[120] *ST*, I, Q. 47, art. 1. You may also recall this quotation from our introductory chapter.
[121] Ibid., Q. 104, art. 1.
[122] Ibid., art. 4.

natures, and of the gifts and fruits of the Holy Spirit, the God-infused theological virtues, and the Beatitudes that enable us to partake of God's divine nature as we sojourn on earth on our way to heaven.[123] Do you seek truly to know and acquire virtue and grace? Then read part II of the *Summa Theologica*!

In part III of the *Summa*, Thomas turns his towering intellect to the Word who took on flesh for our sins, so that we might attain eternal life with Him. It is Christ who mediates the hope for our salvation and ultimate return to and union with God. Here he examines Jesus Christ as the Word, the second person of the Holy Trinity, and also as the man Jesus Christ, Son of the Blessed Virgin. Any who love Christ can deepen their understanding and love of Him by reading part III of the *Summa Theologica*. Thomas also addresses the sacraments there and provides a fascinating analysis of a variety of topics, including the natures of our glorified bodies after the resurrection.

Thomas the thinker brought thought to its earthly heights as it pondered heavenly glory. As great a thinker as Saint Thomas was, he knew very well that God wants us to do and to love as well, and here too Saint Thomas would heed God's call most angelically, gladly sharing with others the fruits of his contemplation.

Angelic Teaching, Writing, and Preaching

Remember the opening verse for this chapter: "From your heights you water the mountains; the earth is filled with the fruits of your works"? By far Saint Thomas's main work as a doer was in the

---

[123] I've done my best to summarize Thomas's presentation of the virtues and gifts in *Unearthing Your Ten Talents* (Sophia Institute Press, 2009) and of sins in *The Seven Deadly Sins* (Sophia Institute Press, 2015), so I won't belabor them here.

role of a *teacher*. This verse, you see, was the scriptural theme of Thomas's inaugural lecture in his role of teacher at the University of Paris in 1256. We are blessed that this lecture is extant,[124] an early example of young Thomas's gifts for moving metaphorical expression along with a penetrating, deep-seated wisdom. Water comes to the mountains from the heavens above, forming rivers that flow down to the earth, giving it life and making it fertile. "Similarly, the minds of teachers, symbolized by the mountains, are watered by the things that are above in the wisdom of God, and by their ministry the light of divine wisdom flows down into the minds of students."[125]

Those mountainous minds of whom Thomas speaks are the teachers of Sacred Scripture who need to be "high" in the quality of their lives, so they, like the prophets and apostles before them, will be able to pass on to others the life-giving rains of God's wisdom. So ardently did this young professor respect and ascend to those mountains of wisdom that he himself would grow into one of the loftiest of all peaks. Thomas would sit in the Dominican chair of philosophy twice in his lifetime and would serve the papacy and the Dominican Order as a teacher and at times as a director of studies for most of the rest of his days. His complete devotion to the Dominican academic mission is seen in this first lecture as well. "These three functions, preaching, teaching and disputing, are mentioned in Titus 1:9, 'So that he will be capable of exhorting people' (this refers to preaching), 'in sound teaching' (this refers to lecturing), 'and of defeating those who contradict' (this refers to disputing.)"[126]

---

[124] See Tugwell, *Albert and Thomas*, 355–360.
[125] Ibid., 355.
[126] Ibid., 358.

Further, despite his heavy teaching loads he would produce as well a mountain of holy writings. In addition to the two great *Summas* already mentioned, Saint Thomas would write complete and engaging commentaries on many books of the Bible, including all the letters of Saint Paul and a particularly sublime commentary on the Gospel of Saint John. He would write extensive articles on many "disputed questions" of the day, including, for example, the nature of virtue. He wrote such masterful line-by-line commentaries on many of the books of the philosopher Aristotle[127] that some have said you can get a better understanding of Aristotle by reading Aquinas than by reading Aristotle himself! Not nearly finished yet, Saint Thomas would also work on a shorter *Compendium of Theology*,[128] explaining in simple terms key ideas from his *Summas*. Organized in three parts under the headings of faith, hope, and charity, it is more than 350 pages long, but Thomas died before it was completed.

Thomas was the most masterful of thinkers, teachers, and writers, for he was gifted by God with a most powerful intellect and always reached out to the source of his wisdom in prayer whenever he studied, wrote, or taught. When it came to other forms of the active life, Thomas was always very hesitant to take on any task that removed him from those main pursuits. Unlike his master Albert, he would decline any positions of authority within the Church and the order that did not involve teaching. Early in his life, he declined the offer to serve as abbot of the Benedictine Monastery of Monte Cassino, even though the pope

---

[127] Saint Thomas refers to Aristotle respectfully as the Philosopher in the pages of the *Summa Theologica*.

[128] Available from Sophia Institute Press as *Aquinas's Shorter Summa*.

was willing to allow him to do so clad in the habit of the Order of Friars Preachers! Later in his life, he would turn down the role of archbishop of Naples. The Angelic Doctor foreshadowed the angelic painter. Fra Angelico would decline high office in preference for his brush as Thomas had done for his lectern and his pen.

Still, every Dominican is called forth to be a doer in a most particular way—that is, of course, in the form of *preaching*—and Thomas, like Albert, did not neglect that call at all. Like the towering Albert, this mountain of wisdom gladly poured forth simple, nourishing streams of God's wisdom for any congregation before him. As he said in his opening lecture, "The teacher ought not to preach all that he knows to simple people, because he himself cannot know all that there is in the mysteries of God."[129] Later in his life, Saint Thomas practiced what he had preached, as he literally preached what he had learned so well! In a series of extremely well-attended Lenten sermons at Naples, Thomas opened up the Creed, the Lord's Prayer, the Hail Mary, and the sacraments in a straightforward and delightful way. Indeed, modern Thomist Ralph McInerny would declare that Thomas's sermons on the Apostles' Creed could be called "a *Summa* for the Simple."[130]

Saint Thomas Aquinas and the Fervent Love of Charity

Saint Thomas reveals the ultimate meaning and significance of Christian love in his writings on the human passion of love

---

[129] Tugwell, *Albert and Thomas*, 359.

[130] Ralph McInerny, foreword to *The Aquinas Catechism: A Simple Explanation of the Catholic Faith by the Church's Greatest Theologian* (Manchester, New Hampshire: Sophia Institute Press, 2000), xii. This book is based on Thomas's Lenten sermons.

and on the God-given theological virtue of charity. In treating of the human passion of love, Thomas argues, in essence, that love really does make the world go 'round! Thomas calls what we commonly refer to as feelings or emotions *passions*. Even though we experience them intensely and they may motivate us to action, Thomas uses the word *passion* because the word implies *passivity*, in the sense that our bodies and souls have *receptivity* — the ability to be influenced by objects outside ourselves, whether to draw us toward them (as in love) or to repel us (as in hate). In a very real way, then, love motivates all our actions, because we constantly seek to obtain what we believe is good. This is why Thomas, echoing Saint Augustine, so flatly stated that "good alone is the cause of love."[131] If we are to become the kind of lovers God intends us to be, then it is of extreme importance that what we *love*, what we *believe* is good for us, really is.

Thomas notes as well that "the inordinate love of self is the cause of every sin."[132] God Himself is the ultimate good and the Creator and Sustainer of every lesser good. We sin when we turn our attention from the good of living a life in accordance with God's will to the good of satisfying our selfish desires. Of course, we are called to love ourselves, but *through* and not *before* or *instead of* our love of God and our neighbor. Christ told us that this was God's greatest commandment of all.[133] And so great is God's love for us that He also gives us the tools through His grace so that we can achieve just that, great joyful love for

---

[131] *ST*, I-II, Q. 27, art. 1.
[132] Ibid., Q. 77, art. 4.
[133] Cf. Matt. 22:35–40; Mark 12:28–31; Luke 10:25–28; Deut. 6:4–5; Lev. 19:18.

Him that is expressed through the love of our neighbors and even of ourselves.

Chief among God's great aids to us is the theological virtue of charity that God infuses in our hearts if we choose to accept the offer of His grace. Love in the sense of charity seeks the highest good—the attainment of union with God. It is here, in his masterful treatise on charity in the *Summa Theologica*,[134] that the Angelic Doctor soared to the heights in some of his most insightful, inspiring, and beautiful analysis of the life of loving charity that God invites us to enjoy with Him.

Saint Thomas begins his lengthy treatise on charity by showing how charity is really a state of *friendship* between man and God, citing 1 Corinthians 1:9: "*God is faithful; by Whom you are called unto the fellowship of His Son.* Love based on this friendship is charity; wherefore it is evident that charity is the friendship of man for God."[135]

The love for that which is good for ourselves is a love of concupiscence (or natural desire) such as we might experience for a fine wine or a favorite horse (Thomas's own examples). In the love of *true* friendship, we love the friend for his own sake and not merely for the fact that he is useful or provides us with pleasure. We rejoice in our friend's existence, want to be with him, and wish the best for him and those dear to him. We not only wish him well but also take actions for his benefit to express that love. What an amazing honor that the Creator of the universe has extended His deepest friendship to each of us! Indeed, not only does God's friendship express His joy *that* we exist; it actually *causes* us to exist!

---

[134] *ST*, II-II, Qs. 23–46.
[135] Ibid., Q. 23, art. 1.

Saint Thomas compares the love of charity to the heat of a powerful furnace. When our hearts burn with the fires of charity, their far-reaching flames serve to warm strangers and even our enemies. But since those closest to the furnace receive the most heat, true charity should begin at home and be directed in greatest intensity to the Spirit who dwells within our hearts, and to those who are near to us — our families, friends, school- or workmates, neighbors, and fellow parishioners. Thomas makes clear that we are indeed called to love *ourselves* and even our *own bodies* with the love of charity.

So how can we fan the flames of the charity God places within our hearts? Although charity, as a theological virtue, is infused in our hearts by God, it can increase or decrease through our actions. Saint Thomas tells us with moving eloquence how each act of charity increases within us the disposition or tendency to more charitable acts, "and this readiness increasing, breaks out into an act of more fervent love, and strives to advance in charity, and then this charity increases actually."[136] Aristotle says that we become builders by building and harpists by playing the harp. Thomas tells us we become fervent lovers by loving fervently!

One of my favorite quotes from Saint Thomas goes as follows: "The love of our neighbor requires that not only should we be our neighbor's well-wishers, but also his well-doers."[137] Charity is a dynamic virtue that acts and works and gets good things done — all through our love for God.

Thomas not only *wrote about* acts of fervent love, but he *lived* and *acted* fervent love of God and neighbor in both the most lofty and the most simple ways. Saint Thomas's ardent desire for

[136] Ibid., Q. 24, art. 6.
[137] Ibid., Q. 32, art. 5; cf. 1 John 3:18.

union with God is seen not only in his theological masterpieces, but in the astoundingly beautiful hymns he wrote to God for the newly established feast of Corpus Christi (the Body of Christ). His "Pange, Lingua, Gloriosi" ("Acclaim, My Tongue, This Mystery"), for example, builds on an ancient hymn in six stanzas with sonorous Latin rhymes expressing the most loving devotion that clearly rings through even in English translations. Here is the first stanza:[138]

Pange, Lingua, Gloriosi	Acclaim, My Tongue, This Mystery
Pange, lingua, gloriosi	Acclaim, my tongue, this mystery
Corporis mysterium	Of glorious Body
Sanguinesque pretiosi,	and precious Blood
Quem in mundi pretium,	Which the King of nations
Fructus ventris generosi,	shed for us
Rex effudit gentium.	A noble womb's sole fruitful bud.

Thomas's fervent love for Christ rings clearly and eloquently in so many of his other hymns as well that every reader should come to know and love them.

Thomas loved his neighbor too in humble and simple ways. He and his friend Brother Reginald of Piperno, O.P., were dear to one another. We owe many of the stories of Saint Thomas's saintly character to the testimony of his dear friend. Loving charity for one's neighbor is always built on a foundation of humility (deriving from *humus*, "earth"), and the mountain of

---

[138] St. Thomas Aquinas, *The Aquinas Prayer Book: The Prayers and Hymns of Saint Thomas Aquinas*, trans. Robert Anderson and Johann Moser (Manchester, NH: Sophia Institute Press, 2000), 88–89.

Thomas's love and wisdom was built on such a lowly, yet sturdy foundation. Consider, for example, that so great was Thomas's love for God's truths that his writings reveal extremely little information about Thomas himself. There are endearing stories of small acts of humility too. The story was told that a new friar came to Thomas's convent and wanted someone to give him a tour around Paris. Thomas was the first friar he saw, and he ordered Thomas to show him around. Thomas obliged the young friar and even put up with complaints that he was walking too slowly. We can only imagine the friar's reaction when he found out later on that the man he took on as a guide and chided was the world's premier theologian!

Thomas was usually very serene and taciturn, although he could get riled up in the defense of important truths. An interesting story is told of his humility even in the face of attacks on his ideas in public and while he was present. A new master of theology at the University of Paris, most likely the Franciscan John Pecham, attacked one of Thomas's philosophical arguments, most likely his position on the philosophical possibility of the eternity of the world, according to Fr. Tugwell.[139] Although all of the university's professors were gathered there, Thomas did not say one word in his defense, explaining later that he did not want to spoil the new master's day!

Feeding Straw to the Furnace of Love

Saint Thomas was a mountain of a man, in body tall and sturdily built, and with a mind that could ascend to the heights. Near the end of his life, on the feast of Saint Nicholas, December 6, 1273, this gentle, angelic giant had an ecstatic experience while saying

---

[139] Tugwell, *Albert and Thomas*, 230.

Mass. The revelation he beheld, perhaps a glimpse of the beatific vision, was so powerful that he told his dear friend Reginald that after what he had seen, he could write no more, since his writings appeared "as straw." Four months later, on March 7, 1274, after a short illness, Thomas died before his fiftieth birthday at the Cistercian monastery at Fossonova.

By calling his writings "straw," Thomas did not renounce them. Thomas had written of three degrees of charity. At the first stage we must fight against sin; at the second stage, we turn our focus to the development of virtue; and in the highest and last stage, we seek only union with God. It was said that Saint Thomas once beheld a vision of Christ. When Christ asked Thomas what he wanted, his answer was "Only You, Lord." Is it possible, then, that near the end of his life, Saint Thomas the lover had broached that third degree of charity, restless for anything but union with God? Could the "straw" that was his theological works have been the kindling that fueled the fires of charity that brought him to that exultant state? May the powerful furnace of Saint Thomas's burning love provide heat for our own loving charity.

Pope Saint Pius V

1504–1572 | FEAST: APRIL 30

Pope Saint Pius V was one of the sons of Saint Dominic who would come to sit in the chair of Saint Peter—and he sure did a lot more than sit there! Anthony Ghislieri was born to poor parents in the town of Bosco in northern Italy. He showed devotion to God, interest in reading, and intellectual precocity from his earliest years, and when some wandering Dominicans wandered by this young shepherd boy, at the age of twelve, he left home to become a hound of the Lord, taking the religious name of Michael. As Saint Michael the Archangel defends us in battle, this Michael would one day do the same in a most spectacular way, with the assistance of the Blessed Mother.

As the years went by and the evidence of his talents and his holiness grew ever more evident, Friar Michael became a bishop, a cardinal, and in 1566 was elected pope. Over the next six years this first-rate thinker became among the most accomplished of all doers. To name just a few of his accomplishments, he would proclaim Saint Thomas Aquinas a Doctor of the Church in 1567. He commissioned the first complete edition of Saint Thomas's works in 1570, the same year he excommunicated Queen Elizabeth I of England for breaking with the Church, and standardized the Mass in the Roman Missal in what became known as the Tridentine Mass, the official Roman rite of the Mass of the Church for the next four hundred years.

Perhaps Pope Pius V is best remembered in his great defense of the Church, of Italy, and all of Europe, when under the protection of the Blessed Mother, he assembled the Holy League, a Christian fleet that on October 7, 1571, decisively defeated an Ottoman navy that sought Muslim dominance over all Europe. Having encouraged all of Christendom to pray the Rosary with him for victory, he declared October 7 the feast of Our Lady of the Rosary.

Saint Catherine's Understanding Penetrates the Heart

> *Blessed are the pure of heart, for they shall see God.*
> —Matthew 5:8
>
> *Understanding denotes a certain excellence of knowledge that penetrates into the heart of things.*
> —Saint Thomas Aquinas, *Summa Theologica*
>
> *I wish you to see the secret of the Heart, showing it to you open, so that you might see how much more I loved than I could show you by finite pain.*
> —Christ to Saint Catherine of Siena, *The Dialogue*

A Female Doctor in Saint Dominic's House

Perhaps it is no surprise that our first two great Dominican thinkers, Saint Albert, the patron of scientists, and Saint Thomas, the patron of scholars, would hold prominent places with the small list of saints (thirty-six to date) officially recognized as Doctors of the Church (from the Latin docere, "to teach"). After all, as Aristotle and Saint Thomas had noted, a sign of one possessing true science or knowledge is the ability to teach. Saint Albert was the greatest teacher of his day who produced the greatest student perhaps of all days, Saint Thomas Aquinas. Who could possibly argue that those two were not indeed great Doctors, "mountains," in Thomas's metaphor, who drink in the rain of God's wisdom and direct it downstream in great rivers of learning to be spread throughout the earth?

The hounds of the Lord have one more illustrious Doctor-teacher in their holy rolls whose achievements and title might seem a bit surprising. This third Doctor is no world-renowned scientist, professor, philosopher, or theologian. This third Doctor is no priest and could never be one. This third Doctor, the twenty-third of twenty-five children, was born not into a noble or knightly family but to a poor dyer of wools and his wife. This third Doctor would not be immersed in the *trivium* and *quadrivium* in youth and indeed would not learn to read until nearly twenty and to write even after that. This Doctor was also a woman and only the second woman named a Doctor of the Church.[140] She would die young, at age thirty-three, the same age as did the Love of her life and her spiritual Spouse, yet any who come to know of her life and her teachings cannot help but agree that between the Great Universal Doctor and the Angelic Doctor rightfully sits the Seraphic Virgin in the high teaching chair that she merited by embracing and sharing Christ's grace.

---

[140] She was declared a Doctor by Pope Paul VI on October 4, 1970. The first woman to be declared a Doctor was Saint Teresa of Ávila just one week before, and joining her since, besides Saint Catherine, are Saint Thérèse of Lisieux and Saint Hildegard of Bingen.

If we were to personify intellectual virtue, who would better represent the virtue of *science* or *knowledge* than Saint Albert the Great, that saintly scientist of encyclopedic knowledge? Who would better personify *wisdom*, the virtue that aims at the loftiest of things and puts everything in order, than Saint Thomas Aquinas, who had, through deep respect, prayer, and study, "inherited the intellect" of all the Church Fathers who had come before him? Now, there are three intellectual virtues, as there are three Dominican Doctors of the Church (thus far!). Who, then, would better personify *understanding*, the virtue that "penetrates into the heart of things" than Saint Catherine of Siena, the Seraphic Virgin,[141] so pure in heart that she was shown and given in mystical ecstasy the very heart of Jesus Christ?

Let's get to know this most unusual teacher as we glance at her life and then strive to penetrate into her heart, the heart of a most ardent thinker, doer, and lover for Christ.

Daughter of a Dyer, Spouse of the One Who Died — and Rose

We are very fortunate in the case of Saint Catherine of Siena because a gifted Dominican writer, indeed, the twenty-third master general of the Order of Preachers, Blessed Raymond of Capua, was Catherine's confessor, friend, follower, and biographer. From his personal experience and correspondence with Catherine, her family, friends, and previous confessors, Blessed Raymond has given this "mini-biographer" of sorts a great wealth of material to choose from. Bear in mind, then, that I provide here but the

---

[141] The seraphim, according to tradition, are the highest order of angels, in closest union with God, known for their light, love, and purity.

smallest sample of episodes from this great saint's life. Readers who thirst for more are directed to Blessed Raymond's 300-plus-page biography.

On the feast of the Annunciation and a Palm Sunday as well, March 25, 1347, in the north-central Tuscany region of Italy, but a stone's throw south of Florence,[142] in the still beautiful and then powerful city of Siena, Italy, was born a child whose birth would bring great joy, mingled with great suffering. The linen and wool dyer Giacomo di Benincasa and his wife, Lapa, would celebrate with joy the births of their twenty-third and twenty-fourth children, twin daughters Catherine and Jane, although only Catherine would survive for more than a few days.

Baby Catherine must have had the lovely, endearing temperament that modern psychologists say characterizes the "easy" child, as opposed to the "difficult" or the "slow-to-warm-up," because family and friends always wanted to "borrow" her for a while! Some report she was given the nickname of Euphrosyne after the ancient mythical Greek muse of merriment or joy. Blessed Raymond believes she chose the name herself, and we'll see why shortly.

Legends report an early spiritual zeal and holiness. From the age of five she would ascend the stairs of the house genuflecting at each step while reciting a Hail Mary. Some said that angels would sometimes carry her up those steps so quickly that it scared Lapa, her mother.

At age six Catherine, who had been out with her brother Stephen, had a vision of Christ above the gable of the Church of Saint Dominic. He was seated on a throne in priestly vestments and crowned with a papal tiara, and He gave her a priestly

---

[142] For those who can toss a stone thirty-one miles.

blessing. When her brother came back to look for her and grabbed her by the arm, the vision had vanished, but its impact clearly did not, for throughout her life Catherine would be absorbed in the things of Christ, His vicar on earth, His priests, and all His holy Church.

At the age of seven, Catherine invoked the Blessed Virgin and promised herself to Christ, declaring she would never marry any other and would live a life of perpetual virginity. This was a secret vow, though, and one of which her mother would not have approved.

For the next few years Catherine grew in devotion and regularly frequented the Dominican Church in Siena. When Catherine reached adolescence, her mother was determined to dress her up, fix her hair, and teach her all the ways for a girl to win a good husband. Catherine showed little interest in such things, so her mother called in Catherine's beloved older married sister Bonaventura. Under her sister's influence, Catherine did devote more time to her appearance for a while until her sister suddenly died in 1362 and God revealed to Catherine that the soul of her sister was suffering in purgatory. Catherine castigated herself for her brief foray into vanity and vowed that never again would she strive to make herself physically attractive to others. Still, Catherine had not revealed her vow of chastity to her mother, and Lapa doubled down in her efforts to find her a husband.

Now is when we see why Blessed Raymond thought Catherine chose the nickname Euphrosyne for herself, because, according to the legend of Saint Euphrosyne of Alexandria, this fifth-century saint dressed as a man to enter a monastery to live a life of celibate asceticism. When Lapa asked a Dominican Father to talk to Catherine, he advised her to cut off her hair to prove the firmness of her holy intentions. Catherine did so in an instant and covered her head with a veil. When her mother snatched the veil from her head, she reacted with ferocious anger and punished Catherine severely. The maid would be relieved of her duties, and Catherine would be required to do all the most menial household tasks so that she would not have the time or energy to pray. They also took away her small room, but this did not daunt Catherine, as she prayed inwardly and constantly while she served the family's needs.

Her father, Giacomo, grew increasingly aware of Catherine's holiness, however, and once as she knelt in prayer, he saw a vision of a dove perched on her head. Catherine too had visions of her own while in ecstatic prayer, and, in one, the heavens opened and the founding saints of various orders appeared and called out to her. She felt no desire to move until a founder who came bearing a beautiful white lily[143] assured her that she would one day wear the habit that her heart desired, a habit of white to symbolize innocence and black to symbolize humility.

This vision gave her the courage to announce to her family the vow of virginity that she had made years ago and to tell them of her desire to become a Dominican. This moved her family, her father first, and he declared that her holy pursuits should be no longer thwarted but aided. Catherine was given a small room of her own, where she prayed and practiced extreme mortifications. She would go on at age sixteen to wear the habit of the Third Order Dominican Mantellate, a group that until her admission consisted only of older widows. Catherine's "Husband" had died too, although He had also risen.

---

[143] A symbol associated with Saint Dominic for his perpetual chastity.

Catherine would spend years in seclusion and prayerful meditations until God told her it was time that she share those fruits born of contemplation and go forth and do great things for Christ, for His poor, His sick, His vicar, His priests, and all of His Church. It's time now to pull out our trifocals of thinking, doing, and loving to take a good look at the mature Catherine, so pure in heart that she saw God, so deep in understanding that she penetrated and shared Christ's Sacred Heart and became His mystical spouse.

Saint Catherine the Thinker Dialogues with Christ

Catherine was contemplative in virtually every sense of the word. If we are to examine and reflect on, to *contemplate*, if you will, Catherine as an exemplar of what we are calling here the *contemplative* spiritual style, we ought to examine just what the word *contemplate* means. The *American Heritage Dictionary* notes it means "1. To look at pensively. 2. To ponder or consider thoughtfully. 3. To intend or anticipate. 4. To regard as possible; take seriously." Synonyms include *ponder* and *meditate*. Quite interestingly, its Latin origin, *contemplari*, "to observe carefully," was based on the ancient practice of augury, and referred to marking off a *templum*, a space from which pagan augurs would carefully observe before making their predictions.

When we contemplate, we set aside a place, either externally in the physical world or interiorly within our minds and hearts, or both, to ponder, observe, and meditate. After Catherine donned the habit of the Mantellate she spent three years in seclusion, except for when she went to church for confession and Mass, in the small room of her family's house that she converted into a *templum* of continual prayer, fasting, silence, self-mortification, and study. Catherine had been inspired since childhood by the prayerful ancient Desert Fathers. Per Blessed Raymond, she "established a desert within the walls of her own home, and solitude in the midst of people."[144]

It is fascinating to consider that it was not until these years of contemplation that this great Doctor of the Church even learned to read and write! Blessed Raymond reports that she wanted to read so she could say the Divine Praises and the Canonical Hours, but the efforts of a friend to teach her the alphabet didn't get far after several weeks. During a prayer one morning, Catherine asked Christ to teach her so that she could say the Psalms and sing His prayers, since she was not smart enough to master it on her own, adding that she would remain ignorant and meditate on Him in other ways if this was not His will. When she arose, she found she could read fluently. Raymond noted that she read so fast that she was not able to read out separate syllables and could hardly spell the words, which he took as a sign of a miracle. Catherine read Latin but could not speak it. She would not go on to write her first letter until 1377 at around the age of thirty. Her ability to write came as a gift in a vision of Christ, who was accompanied by His beloved disciple Saint John and the Angelic Doctor, Saint Thomas Aquinas. Her letters and *Dialogue* were written in Italian and in such beautiful language that they have been compared to the works of Dante.

During these years of secluded contemplation and through the remainder of her life as well, Saint Catherine experienced many mystical ecstasies with visions of Christ and of the saints. Raymond relates an early vision of Christ in which the most

---

[144] Blessed Raymond of Capua, *The Life of Saint Catherine of Siena* (Charlotte, NC: Saint Benedict Press, 2006), 54.

profound of theological proofs are stated simply and sublimely in just a handful of words. Read the first part of Saint Thomas's *Summa Theologica*, and you will find page after page of reasoned argumentation leading to the inevitable conclusion that God must exist, indeed that His, and only His, essence and existence are one. This is summed up in but a few words in the name God Himself revealed at Moses' prompting: "I AM WHO I AM" (Exod. 3:14). Jesus would recapitulate this profound truth Himself when He declared, "Truly, truly, I say to you, before Abraham was, I am" (John 8:58).

In one of Saint Catherine's first visions, Christ asked of her, "Do you know, daughter, who you are, and who I am? If you know these two things, you will be blessed. You are she who is not; whereas I am He who is."[145] These simple words were as a *Summa* enriching Catherine's growth in wisdom and understanding. As Blessed Raymond explains, "All creatures are engulfed in nothingness — made from nothingness, tending toward nothingness."[146] Sin is a nothingness, a lack of a goodness that should be present, so that when we sin, we move back toward nothingness. This is why Christ said, "[A]part from me you can do nothing" (John 15:5) and why Saint Paul said, "I can do all things in him who strengthens me" (Phil. 4:13). We must embrace humility in the recognition of our potential nothingness and the fervent love of charity for the One who gives us life and sustains us.

Among the most profound of Catherine's ecstatic visions was the "mystical marriage" in which she was espoused to Christ, the wedding party including the Virgin Mother, Saint John the

---

[145] Ibid., 62.
[146] Ibid., 63.

Evangelist, Saint Paul, Saint Dominic, and King David, who played his harp. Christ presented her a ring that was invisible to others, but which she could see for the rest of her life. In another most powerful vision revealed to her confessor, she asked Christ to take her own heart and will from her, and Christ came to her and removed her heart. Some days later, he appeared to her again and placed his own heart within her breast. Saint Thomas said that understanding is an excellence of knowledge that penetrates into the heart of things. Christ Himself said that the pure of heart shall see God. Through the Holy Spirit's gift of understanding, Catherine was given visions of Christ, and in a mystical sense, His very own Sacred Heart.[147]

The fruits of Catherine's gifts of understanding blossomed most completely in her dictated work called *The Dialogue* or *The Dialogue of Divine Providence*,[148] in which Catherine makes four requests to God the Father for herself, for the Church, for the world, and for assurance of His divine providence to provide for all things. The responses come from God in four treatises of over two hundred pages on divine providence, discretion, prayer, and obedience. The *Dialogue* treats of a great many basic, essential, creedal, catechetical issues of faith and morals in the most moving, intimate, and creative ways. They drip with moving and memorable metaphors containing great mystical truths. So many of the lessons speak of love; we will save those for our

---

[147] For those moved by religious art in the spirit of Fra Angelico, I direct you to a depiction of this mystical exchange of hearts by Sienese artist Giovani di Paolo (1398–1482). Saint Catherine in her black and white Dominican habit clutches a red, bleeding heart, while Christ speaks to her from within a cloud of gold.

[148] She never gave it a title herself, calling it simply "The Book."

section on Saint Catherine as a lover. Here I'll merely highlight
a few of each treatise of *The Dialogue*'s main themes and images.

A Treatise on Divine Providence. Catherine speaks of "the virtue
of desire," of the soul's "fire of holy desire" that makes us con-
trite of heart for our sins and desirous of the limitless loving
mercy of God, made possible for us through Christ's Crucifixion. Our holy desire brings remission of sins, and here our holy
hound of the Lord speaks of the "hound of conscience" as well:
"I wake up in them the hound of conscience, and make them
smell the odor of virtue, and take delight in the conversation
of My servants."[149]

She provides insights as well on the nature of virtues and of
suffering and injuries, noting the virtues are demonstrated and
fortified by their contraries. Patience, for example, is proven
and fortified when one is injured by his neighbor. It is through
such injuries that patience is given the opportunity to mani-
fest itself and grow. We build justice within our souls when we
are treated unjustly. The virtue of humility is proved by and
conquers the vice of pride, because a proud person can do no
harm to the humble, who are not concerned about their worldly
reputation. God, in his providence, has so arranged the world
that from vices in some spring virtues in others; from contrition
for sin springs limitless mercy; from worldly suffering springs
heavenly joy.

A Treatise of Discretion. Here Saint Catherine reveals the Dominican thirst to bring souls to Christ. God tells her our works are
holy and sweet to Him when they are infused "with hunger and

---

[149] Saint Catherine of Siena, *The Dialogue*, no. 7.

desire for My honor and the salvation of souls."[150] Here, too, she explicates on the instrument through which God provided the mechanism for our salvation in her most famous metaphorical elaboration of Christ as the Bridge by which man can pass from earth into heaven. This Bridge has three "steps" that signify the three states of the soul[151] through which we ascend to heaven from earth. The first step signifies "the feet of the soul,"[152] representing our affections, because as the feet carry the body, so do our desires and affections carry our soul. The pierced feet of Christ the Bridge are the means by which we reach the second step, at His side, which reveals to us the secret of His heart. When the soul desires to taste the love of Christ's heart and gazes into his heart with the eye of the intellect, it finds His heart "consumed with ineffable love."[153] Having tasted of this love, the soul reaches the third step, of Christ's mouth, and finally attains peace from the terrible war that it has waged against sin. In the first step, then, the soul steps away from earthly affections and is stripped of vice. In the second step, the soul fills itself with love and virtue. In the third step, the soul "tastes peace."[154] So then this Bridge to heaven was lifted on high for us when the Father's Son was lifted up on the wood of the holy Cross, "the Divine nature remaining joined to the lowliness of the earth of your humanity."[155]

---

[150] *The Dialogue*, 19.

[151] Saint Catherine also explicitly relates them to the three powers of the soul of memory, intellect, and will, according to Saint Augustine, reflections in the soul of man of the Holy Trinity.

[152] *The Dialogue*, 40.

[153] Ibid.

[154] Ibid.

[155] Ibid.

A Treatise of Prayer. Saint Thomas Aquinas had written that prayer is a most reasonable thing to do. Citing the ancient Roman theologian Cassiodorus, Thomas had agreed that "prayer is spoken reason"[156] and that speech is a function of the *intellect*, a power that no other creature on earth has been given by God. Prayer, for Thomas, was "the raising of one's mind to God,"[157] and the "parts" of prayer include *supplications* (humble requests) for particular blessings from God and *thanksgiving* for blessings He has already provided.

Saint Catherine provides most penetrating insights on the relationship between the intellect, the Scriptures, and the life of prayer. "The intellect was, before the Scriptures were formed, wherefore, from the intellect came science, because in seeing they discerned."[158] God illuminated the intellects of the ancient prophets and apostles before all the Scriptures had been written down. Likewise, after we had received the Holy Scriptures, God gave light to the eyes of the intellect of holy, prayerful men, such as Thomas Aquinas, Augustine, and Jerome, so that even the light that comes from Holy Scriptures comes through the supernatural light of illumination. God warns us, then, that we would be better off seeking spiritual counsel from a holy person of upright conscience than from a proud, learned person who lacks God's supernatural light. Those without God's light are mired in the darkness of self-love, which is "a tree on which nothing grows but fruits of death, putrid flowers, stained leaves, branches bowed down, and struck by various winds."[159] Indeed, the seven deadly sins are this tree's seven drooping branches. They droop

[156] *ST*, II-II, Q. 83, art. 1.
[157] Ibid., art. 17.
[158] *The Dialogue*, 119.
[159] Ibid., 132.

to the earth because only earthly things can feed them, and they are never satisfied. Man has been placed not below but above all other creatures, though, and he cannot be satisfied except when he rests with the eternal God.

A Treatise of Obedience. Here Saint Catherine sails into the theological waters of obedience to God's will, for all of us in general and in particular for those of religious orders who have taken vows of obedience, chastity, and poverty. She compares the religious orders to great ships that sail toward the port of salvation. These ships are so rich that the religious need not worry about their temporal or their spiritual needs, for those who are obedient will receive all they need through the Holy Spirit who guides them.

"Now look at the ship of your Father Dominic,"[160] God tells her. That ship was ordered perfectly, since Saint Dominic wished only that his sons would endeavor to bring honor to God and seek the salvation of souls, "with the light of science," which is the order's principal foundation. It cherishes poverty too, not as an end in itself, but so that the preachers need not be distracted by temporal things as they fight error and spread God's truths. The three riggings of obedience, chastity, and poverty make his a royal ship and make it broad, joyous, and fragrant. Glorious sons of the order Saints Thomas and Peter Martyr are praised for the illumination that arose from their obedience, and Dominic's friend in Christ is praised for his order too: "Of a truth Dominic and Francis were two columns of the holy Church. Francis with the poverty which was especially his own, as has been said, and Dominic with his learning."[161]

[160] *The Dialogue*, 205.
[161] Ibid., 208.

Saint Catherine the Doer Brings Christ's Vicar Back Home

In the *Treatise of Discretion,* we read that God the Father told Catherine, "I take delight in few words and many works."[162] Saint Catherine took those words and ran with them as few others have done. It was not long after her spiritual espousal that Jesus instructed Catherine to leave the room of her private hermitage and rejoin her family at the table as a first step into the active life. As Raymond of Capua so eloquently put it, commenting on both the Song of Solomon and Catherine's introduction to the active life, "He awakens His spouse from her sleep on the bed of contemplation, where she had been lying unmindful of temporal things."[163] Christ told her she must walk with the feet of the love of God and the love of neighbor and "with two wings fly to heaven."[164] When Catherine "woke up," she walked with both feet and prepared herself for flight, vigorously pursuing the active life, tending to the physical and spiritual needs of her neighbors with tireless abandon.

Catherine began her public life of good works doing the most menial of housework, often experiencing mystical ecstasies as she prayed while she worked. She left the home too, and her group of friends and followers grew and came to call this young woman still in her twenties but graced in wisdom beyond her years by the nickname of Mamma. She embarked on projects of providing alms and goods to the poor. Having embraced poverty, she did this at first with her father's possessions and with his permission.

---

[162] Ibid., 23.

[163] Blessed Raymond of Capua, *The Life of Saint Catherine of Siena,* 87.

[164] Ibid., 90.

She took particular care in addressing the needs of the sick, and we'll examine one of the most powerful stories of the way that she nursed those most sickly and most despised when we look at her next as a lover.

Catherine became a doer as well on the largest of scales, truly a mover and shaker in the whole world of Christendom. Her century, the fourteenth, was as full of sorrows and trials for the Church and the world as Albert and Thomas's, the thirteenth, was full of joys and triumphs. Hers was a century of devastating plagues that decimated populations, including her own Siena, of corruption and schism within the Church, of wars between Church and states and between neighboring cities within the European continent, all in the face of ongoing threats from the Muslim Turks. Nonetheless, this slight, young, uneducated hound of the Lord played among the greatest of roles in restoring health, wholeness, and holiness in such a blighted time. Indeed, in future centuries she would come to be known as the Doctor of Unity and, along with Saint Francis, co-patron of Italy.

Catherine became a great writer of letters to cardinals, popes, and public officials, always seeking peace by encouraging recipients to do the will of God. Her greatest and best-known triumph was to bring the pope back to Rome. Deriving from conflicts between the papacy and the French crown, when Clement V, a Frenchman, was elected pope in 1305, he declined to move to Rome and, in 1309, set up court in the fortified city of Avignon, France. He and the next six popes stayed in Avignon for the next sixty-seven years, until the letters and face-to-face admonitions of Catherine of Siena convinced Pope Gregory XI to bring the papacy home to Rome. Blessed Raymond notes that she had discerned a secret vow Gregory had made upon his papal ascension to return with his court to Rome. Sources report that when

Gregory, then in his forties, made up his mind to leave Avignon behind, he did so against his father's will, indeed literally stepping over his prostrate body on his way out!

Gregory and his successor, Pope Urban VI, elected on April 8, 1378, were well aware of Catherine's gifts of persuasion and would call on her to act as peacemaker in serious disputes, including one in Florence, where she was nearly martyred. So vehement was Pope Urban VI in his sweeping reforms of corruption in the Church that by September 20 of that year, the French cardinals had declared his election invalid and named their own pope, known today as the antipope Clement VII. This began the Western Schism within the Church, during which a pope in Rome and an antipope (or even two) ruled in Avignon and elsewhere. The schism would not end until 1417, twenty-seven years after Catherine's death, but during her lifetime she championed the true papacy of Pope Urban VI.

The virtues of the active life include the cardinal virtues of temperance, fortitude, justice, and prudence, and all of these Catherine possessed in the most heroic degree, having been granted by God the most extraordinary of graces. Catherine's temperance, or self-control, exceeded all earthly bounds. As she progressed through her life, her diet grew sparser and sparser; first she forsook meat, then bread, and then vegetables until it got to the point at which she consumed only the Eucharist and a little water, noting that food made her ill and only the Eucharist gave her strength. She also possessed the temperate virtues of chastity and purity, remaining innocent throughout her life.

Catherine's fortitude was also incomparable. Through the spiritual strength of fortitude we obtain difficult and arduous goods. The highest crown of fortitude is martyrdom, in which one faces the most difficult of things to obtain the highest of goods. Catherine willingly faced martyrdom by the sword once in Florence, but its wielder turned away. Blessed Raymond has noted that by her extreme self-mortifications of abstinence from food, of neglect of sleep (often traveling and working twenty hours per day), and of self-mortifications such as wearing a tight iron chain around her waist, she was in a way a martyr for Christ at the time of her death.

Justice gives each person his rightful due, and Saint Catherine was possessed with giving every person even more than his rightful due, that being salvation and eternal bliss with God. To achieve such means requires great prudence, or practical wisdom, and this too Catherine displayed in superabundance. Prudence finds the right means to virtuous ends, and Catherine almost always found ways to get what she wanted (bearing in mind that *her* wants were whatever God told her He wanted).

Catherine, as we have seen, was a contemplative thinker of the first rank, and a world-class doer, as well. Her thinking and doing were exceeded perhaps only by the loving that drove them.

Saint Catherine the Lover Would Love All Our Souls into Heaven

We will now examine Saint Catherine as a lover in two senses, first as a mystical theologian of love, passing on God's own loving thoughts about what love really means, and secondly, as a real-live human lover, sharing God's love with her neighbor, no matter how apparently insignificant or repugnant that neighbor might be.

The theme of God's loving charity is interwoven throughout all four treatises of *The Dialogue*. In his treatment of the eleven human passions, Saint Thomas noted that "desire" is an attraction to a good not yet attained, of a love not yet fulfilled. In her *Treatise of Divine Providence*, God tells Saint Catherine of the importance of "the virtue of desire" that we must enkindle within our hearts. When Saint Paul wrote that all good works and gifts are naught without love (1 Cor. 13), he instructed us to light the fires of holy desire within our hearts, so that all we do may be motivated by God's love. Further, all sin arises from self-love, rather than love of God and neighbor. God has given us our neighbors as a means to show our love for Him, and this love should be displayed especially to those "close at hand, under your eyes, as to whom, I say, you are all obliged to help one another by word and doctrine, and the example of good works, and in every other respect in which your neighbor may be seen to be in need."[165] So important is this love of neighbor that the Father spelled it for her in these thought- and love-provoking words:

> I could easily have created men possessed of all that they should need both for body and soul, but I wished that one should have need of the other, and that they should be My ministers to administer the graces and the gifts that they have received from Me.[166]

In the *Treatise of Discretion*, Catherine includes a poignant passage on the boundless mercy of God's love for us. God stands ready to forgive absolutely any sin we commit if we come to Him sincerely seeking forgiveness. The worst sin, then, is the despair that deprecates God's loving mercy.

> Therefore is this last sin graver to Me than all other sins that the soul has committed. Wherefore the despair of

[165] *The Dialogue*, 12.
[166] Ibid., 16.

Judas displeased Me more, and was more grave to My Son than was his betrayal of Him.[167]

In the *Treatise of Prayer* God reiterates the theme that we can never adequately repay Him with the love that we owe Him for forming and upholding our very existence, which is why He has given us our neighbors, as a medium through whom we can love Him and serve Him, so we should love our neighbor with the same pure love with which He has loved us, seeking our neighbor's good without seeking our own profit.

Finally, in the *Treatise of Obedience*, Catherine reminds us of the joy that is the desire of love fulfilled:

> Thus the conversations of a truly obedient man are good and perfect, whether they be with just men or with sinners, through his rightly ordered love and the breadth of his charity. Of his cell he makes a heaven, delighting there to converse with Me, his supreme and eternal Father, with the affection of love.[168]

We will remember that God had told Catherine that He prefers deeds to words, and for every word she wrote about love of God and neighbor, she performed countless loving deeds for the least of the people close at hand and right under her eyes. I'll end, then, by briefly recounting just one astonishing case of selfless love that Saint Catherine provided to one of the many hospital patients under her care.

The case concerns one Andrea, a fellow Sister of Penance of Saint Dominic (a Mantellate) who had advanced breast cancer. She bore a festering open wound on her chest that emitted such a

---

[167] *The Dialogue*, 59.
[168] Ibid., 212.

stench that few would go near her to care for her. Raymond tells us that when Catherine heard of Andrea's plight, "she realized that heaven had reserved this unfortunate woman especially for herself"[169] and immediately sought her out. Catherine treated her wounds day after day in a warm and affectionate spirit. One day, however, when she opened the wound's dressing, as Blessed Raymond puts it, since the devil was unable to assault Catherine's will, he assaulted her through her stomach, and she felt a great wave of nausea. Catherine struggled with herself, chiding herself for her disgust for the sister, and forcing herself to consider that she, who had been saved by the blood of Christ, could herself be afflicted with such a disease or worse.

Recall, if you will, the quotation from Saint Albert the Great that appeared in this book's preface: "The roving dogs are the Order of Preachers who do not wait at their homes for the poor but go out to them and lick the ulcers of their sins having in their mouths the bark of preaching." Albert was providing a metaphorical interpretation of Luke 16:19–21. Saint Catherine, on the other hand, when her nausea was quelled, moved from the metaphorical to the literal, for this hound of the Lord literally licked the ulcer of her patient, forcing her mouth upon the wound to overcome the devil and conquer her disgust.

After this incident in which the devil failed, he had some success with the patient, Andrea herself, who became abusive to Catherine and began to spread lies dishonoring Catherine's purity. Catherine continued to care for her all the while and instantly forgave her when she eventually asked for the saint's forgiveness.

---

[169] Blessed Raymond of Capua, *The Life of Saint Catherine of Siena*, 121.

Another gruesome act of fortitude, self-conquering, and love would follow when Catherine felt nauseated again one day while cleaning Andrea's wound. Chiding herself once again, she picked up the bowl that had been used to wash the sore and gulped down its fetid contents. Her sense of repugnance left her for good, and she would later tell Raymond that she had never tasted anything sweeter. Christ would reward Catherine for her extreme self-mortification in the name of neighborly love, granting her a mystical experience in which she drank from His side.

Few of us could ever hope to match the extremes to which Saint Catherine subdued her will and even her bodily functions and reflexes in the services of Christ, but then again, we were not given her special gifts. We can still learn from her to act out the love we should harbor in our hearts even for all those we encounter who are in need. Although their bodily infirmities or spiritual faults may be repugnant to us, none are unworthy. As Saint Catherine told us clearly through both her words and deeds, each and every person is a medium through whom we love God.

Venerable Louis of Granada

1505–1588 | FEAST: DECEMBER 31

In chapter 8 we will meet the Patroness of the Americas, and we will see that when she sought spiritual nourishment, it was to the fruitful pages of the books of Venerable Louis of Granada that Saint Rose of Lima turned, and in particular to his *Book of Prayer and Meditation*.

Louis was born to poor parents in Granada in the South of Spain. He joined the Dominicans at age nineteen and grew famous for the power of his preaching and for his simple, ascetical style of life. He would decline offers of a bishopric, an archbishopric, and a cardinalate. At age thirty-five he was asked to write that book of spiritual direction from which Saint Rose and countless others have derived such benefit. He would go on to publish forty-five works in Latin, Spanish, and Portuguese and is perhaps best known for his classic, *The Sinner's Guide*. Are we not all sinners after all, in dire need of holy guidance? I was struck myself both by his common sense and by the uncommon zeal of his charity. When I wrote *The Seven Deadly Sins*, I started the chapter on envy with Venerable Louis's words, so worthy of repetition, meditation, and application every day:

> When you envy the virtue of another you are your own
> greatest enemy; for if you continue in a state of grace,
> united to your neighbor through charity, you have a share

in all his good works, and the more he merits, the richer you become. So far, therefore, from envying his virtue, you should find it a source of consolation. Alas! Because your neighbor is advancing, will you fall back? Ah! If you would love him in the virtues which you do not find in yourself, you would share in them through charity; the profit of his labors would also become yours.[170]

[170] Louis of Granada, *The Sinner's Guide* (Veritas Splendor Publications, 2012), 289.

PART 3

Dominican Lovers and the Charitable Style

*Put on then, as God's chosen ones, holy and beloved,
compassion, kindness, lowliness, meekness, and patience,
forbearing one another and, if one has a complaint against another,
forgiving each other; as the Lord has forgiven you,
so you must also forgive. And over all these put on love,
which binds everything together in perfect harmony.*
—Colossians 3:12–14

Saint Martin de Porres's Love Brings Us Together in Christ

He excused the faults of others. He forgave the bitterest injuries, convinced that he deserved much severer punishments on account of his own sins. He tried with all his might to redeem the guilty; lovingly he comforted the sick; he provided food, clothing and medicine for the poor; he helped, as best he could, farm laborers and Negroes, as well as mulattoes, who were looked upon at that time as akin to slaves: thus he deserved to be called by the name the people gave him: "Martin of Charity."
—Pope Saint John XXII

Compassion, my dear Brother, is preferable to cleanliness. Reflect that with a little soap I can easily clean my bed covers, but even with a torrent of tears I would never wash from my soul the stain that my harshness toward the unfortunate would create.
—Saint Martin de Porres

We Can All Be Lovers

The hounds of the Lord come in all breeds and varieties, in pedigrees and "mutts," thanks be to God, who creates and sustains them! So far, we have examined great Dominican "doers" and "thinkers" from the Old World of Catholic Christendom in Europe. The first two of our "lovers" take us into the New World of the Americas and into a new focus on the kind of saints who are known less for ideas, accomplishments, and miracles that founded or reformed movements and shook up the world on a grand scale, as they are for that simple, one-on-one personification of "active love and tenderness," as psychologist Henri Joly put it.

Perhaps most of us have the self-knowledge to realize that we certainly lack the zeal, prudence, and spiritual wherewithal ever to found, like Saint Dominic de Guzman, a great religious family like the Order of Preachers. (Thankfully, he has already done that for us.) Who among us would dare to imagine that he could master the teaching of science of our day like Saint Albert or understand the far-reaching implications of the great ancient philosophers that so far exceeded their own long grasp in the way that Saint Thomas did? As for Catherine of Siena, who among us can imagine exercising such amazing self-control and self-mortification while producing profound theology and reshaping world events for the better? These towering saints shower us with their great gifts, but surely we realize that our own gifts are most likely of a far less extraordinary scale.

We can't all be God's geniuses or movers and shakers of heaven and earth who change the world on a global scale, but every single one of us has the capacity to *love* if we simply accept the charity God infuses in our hearts and strive to make it grow by sharing it with others. Our "lovers" show us how to do this, not in the orders they founded, in their great theological treatises, or in their influence on world events, but in how they turned the simple and ordinary duties of their daily lives into hymns to God's glory and acts of mercy and love to all those they encountered. When we read of their lives, we can *think*, "I *can* do that! I *should* do that!" And then, by God, get out there and *do* that, with *love*.[171]

Scholars, astronomers, natural scientists, artists, and nurses need their patron saints, and so do barbers, hairstylists, gardeners, florists, students, young people, and athletes.[172] Indeed, we all do, and regardless of our calling in life, there is probably a hound of the Lord we can look to for help and inspiration to make whatever we do an instrument of God's love. Indeed, our

---

[171] If you will excuse an embarrassing but true little story, just this morning my wife told me her tasks for the day included cleaning the toilets. As I reclined in my recliner, coffee in one hand, Saint Martin de Porres biography in the other, I told her of the amazing coincidence that I had just read one of the many little stories of Saint Martin de Porres. He had been staying for a time at the palace of the Archbishop of Mexico, who had sought Martin out for the healing of an illness. When a friar found Martin in their priory scrubbing toilets, he asked "Brother Martin, is it not better to be in the house of the Lord Archbishop of Mexico than in the toilets of the convent?" Martin quoted from one of the psalms, "I would rather be a doorkeeper in the house of my God than live in the tents of wickedness" (Ps. 84:10). He then added his own paraphrase, "Father Juan, I prefer a little time spent in this work than many days spent in the House of the Lord Archbishop." Brian J. Pierce, O.P., *Martin de Porres: A Saint of the Americas* (Liguori, MO: Liguori Press, 2004), 16. Anyway, after I told my wife this story, she said *I* could help clean the toilets today! (Saint Martin de Porres, pray for me.)

[172] Among their many patronages, Saint Thomas's includes scholars, Saint Dominic's includes astronomers, Saint Albert's includes scientists, Blessed Fra Angelico's includes artists, Saint Catherine's includes nurses, Saint Martin's includes barbers and hairstylists, Saint Rose's includes gardeners and florists, and Blessed Pier Giorgio's includes students, youths, and athletes.

first great Dominican "lover" is a man who is often depicted in painting and statuary brandishing merely a broom.

The "Mulatto Dog" of the Lord

Martin de Porres was born on December 9, 1579,[173] and died on November 3, 1639, more than 375 years ago now. He was beatified by Pope Gregory XVI in 1837 and canonized by Pope John XXIII in 1962. The illegitimate son of the blue-eyed Spanish *hidalgo*[174] Juan de Porres and one Anna Vazquez, a freed slave of African heritage, he is known primarily for his great works of service and mercy to the sick and the poor and is the patron saint of Peru, of mixed-raced people, of those seeking racial harmony, of public health, of public education, of social justice, and indeed, as was mentioned before, of barbers and hairstylists!

Martin's baptismal certificate noted he was "of an unknown father," indicating that his father did not own up to his paternity at first. Two years later, though, Anna bore Juan a daughter, Juana, and in 1586 their father took them both to Guayaquil, Ecuador, where he held a government post, so they could receive education. Martin and Anna stayed close throughout their lives, and Martin returned home to Lima first, after only a year or so. There Martin's father had arranged for him, from about the age of eight, to live in the home of Isabel Garcia Michel in the poor neighborhood of Malambo, where many African and Creoles of mixed descent lived.

---

[173] At least that's the date of his baptismal certificate at the Church of San Sebastian in Lima, Peru. His birth date might have been different.

[174] A member of the knightly class devoted to the King of Spain.

Martin was likely confirmed by Archbishop (and later Saint) Turibius Mongrovejo, who was a staunch defender of the rights of the native people of Peru, many of whom were harshly treated by their European Christian conquerors.[175]

At the age of twelve or so, Martin became an apprentice to Marcel de Rivero at his barbershop. There he learned to cut hair, trim beards, and wax mustaches but also to diagnose and treat injuries and diseases with herbal medicines and minor surgeries. The barbers of those days were also pretty much surgeons, dentists, pharmacists, and nurses as well. He acquired skills there he would use in God's service for the rest of his life.

During those years Martin also frequently visited the nearby Dominican Church, spent his evenings in prayer, and grew devout in his faith, with special devotions to the Crucified Christ and to the Blessed Virgin Mary.[176] At the age of fifteen, in 1594, he entered the Priory of Our Lady of the Holy Rosary (also known as the Convent of Saint Dominic) in Lima, to become a *donado*, a lay brother of the Third Order who would live with

---

[175] Sadly, for example, a priest recounted the story of Hatuey, a native chief of Cuba, who in 1521, when about to be burned at the stake by Spanish soldiers who had captured him in battle, was asked by that priest if he would accept Christian baptism. The chief asked if men such as these Christian soldiers would be in heaven, and when told that they would be, he replied that he would rather go somewhere else then, where he would not be around such cruel people. Among the most outspoken defenders of the native peoples in those years was the Dominican friar Bartolome de las Casas (1484–1566), author of the telling and influential history *A Short Account of the Destruction of the Indies*.

[176] One of Martin's few personal possessions was a picture of the Blessed Mother.

his Dominican brothers but without taking vows. The donado was the humblest of vocations, and stories tell that Martin's father protested at some point and insisted that Martin be made a religious brother. Martin was content to remain a donado, performing simple deeds of service for the rest of his life, but records show that later, on June 2, 1603, Martin did profess the religious vows of chastity and poverty and became, as his extant signature shows, "Brother Martin de Porras."

Martin lived the simple life of a religious brother for the rest of his life, until November 3, 1639, when his soul left the ring of Dominican brothers praying over him and ascended to join Christ, His Blessed Mother, and the other saints in heaven.

Saint Martin de Porres: Thinker

Saint Martin is not known as an intellectual, or a thinker per se, but we know that God has called us all to think and do and love for Him, and Martin would never neglect a call from God.

Martin's magnificent humility was clearly not built on mental simplicity. He was a man so loving that countless stories about him have been told (and collected) by the people who knew and loved him, and many speak both of his practical wisdom and of his surprisingly sound grasp of abstract theological principles.

If we turn to the intellectual virtue of *science*, we will recall that it entails the grasp of relationships of causes and effects, of how things work and why. We see this in the most direct sense in Martin's swift grasp of the principles of medicine, pharmacy, and surgery. He was a very gifted healer, and during the proceedings on his beatification, there were all kinds of stories of his healings of all sorts of ailments. As we noted, he apprenticed with a barber-surgeon at age twelve, and soon people sought out his services even over those of his mentor.[177]

Invoking now the second intellectual virtue of understanding, Saint Thomas once wrote that some people understand things more deeply than others, "as one who carries a conclusion to its first principles and ultimate causes understands it better than one who reduces it to its proximate causes."[178] At a higher level of analysis, then, regarding Saint Martin's gift for healing, his understanding went deeper than the principles of the medical science of his day, since he attributed the ultimate causation of all his healing to God. In fact, some of the witnesses for his canonization testified that he would use medicines or other techniques to make it *appear* they produced the healing when it was really his touch and his prayer, working through the power of God. One man, for example, talked about an abscess in his mouth that would not heal. Martin packed it with dry string. The pain subsided and the patient was able to sleep. When he awoke in the morning completely without pain, he removed the string and found it completely dry without any signs of blood.

Further, as we have seen, Saint Thomas has called understanding "a certain excellence of knowledge that penetrates into the heart of things." Saint Martin certainly displayed this excellence of knowledge, since he saw each of his patients not only as an illness or a limb or even as a mind-body whole, but as a child of God. He aimed with all his healings not only to cure bodies, but to draw souls closer to Christ.

---

[177] Indeed, meticulous readers of footnotes will recall that later in his life, the Archbishop of Mexico would seek Brother Martin out in hopes of cure of an illness.

[178] *ST*, I, Q. 85, art. 7.

Wisdom is the highest of the intellectual virtues. It judges both the principles of understanding and the causes and effects of science, and it focuses on what matters most, which to Saint Martin was the things of God. Although Saint Martin did not have a university or seminary education,[179] he very generously supported the seminary students, making sure they had adequate supplies such as paper, pens, inks, and books. He was quite literate and reportedly studied the Bible, the lives of the saints, especially the Dominicans Dominic, Vincent Ferrer, and Catherine of Siena, as well as the works of theologians, especially Saint Thomas Aquinas.

One fascinating anecdote relates how two seminary students were debating what they learned in a lecture about Saint Thomas's position on the perfection of essence and existence in God. They reportedly asked Martin, who happened to be passing by, having just swept some room. He responded, "Does not Saint Thomas say that existence is more perfect than essence, but that in God they are one?"[180] Another time two students were opining on a question raised by Saint Thomas, when Martin asked them why they were getting so excited about the issue, since Saint Thomas himself had resolved it. He then proceeded to cite them the question and article numbers in the *Summa Theologica*.

Saint Albert the Great once wrote as follows:

One should bear in mind the difference between the contemplation of faithful Catholics and that of pagan philosophers, for the contemplation of the philosophers

---

[179] Indeed, civil and Church laws of the time prohibited such education for men of mixed race.

[180] See *ST*, I, Q. 3, art. 4.

is for the perfection of the contemplator himself, and consequently it is confined to the intellect and their aim in it is intellectual knowledge. But the contemplation of the Saints, and of Catholics, is for the love of him, that is, of the God they are contemplating.[181]

Martin was clearly no pagan philosopher but a faithful Catholic and a saint (and a Dominican saint at that). Any of Martin's contemplation was inspired by and focused on the love of God.

We see this in his devotion to prayer. One of the earliest stories of his childhood relates how one night he asked Isabel Garcia for a candle or even the smallest remnants of one. Curiosity getting the best of her after a while, she peeked into the boy's room and found him among the flickering shadows, kneeling in prayer before an image of the crucified Christ. Later in his life, Martin's love of Christ, like Saint Catherine's, would show forth in intense dedication to the Eucharist. Saint Catherine sought daily Communion and would often go into hours-long ecstasies in public after her reception of Christ. Often after Martin received Holy Communion, he would be nowhere to be found. His friends and brothers report that Martin sought silence and solitude at these times and had many hiding places throughout the priory, including in dank basements and on the roof. There, in ecstasy, he would contemplate the body, blood, soul, and divinity of the Christ who had given Himself to him. Martin himself never spoke of these ecstasies, and some have opined that his superiors encouraged him not to do so, lest he be suspected of heresy and brought before the Inquisition.

---

[181] Saint Albert the Great, *On Cleaving to God* (Grand Rapids, MI: Lamp Post Books, 2008), 32–33.

Saint Martin de Porres: Doer

"Be doers of the word, and not hearers only" (James 1:22). This was a message Saint Martin took to heart, and what did this consummate doer strive to do? In Christ's words, according to Saint Mark, Christians are to "go into all the world and preach the gospel to the whole creation" (16:15). Dominicans, of course, especially take this to heart, and since Martin was a lay Dominican brother, he did not formally preach homilies, but by his words and deeds he did indeed preach the gospel to countless numbers even to our day.

This was Saint Martin's burning objective, the salvation of souls, and the menial tasks of scrubbing toilets and sweeping floors, along with healing the sick and providing for the needs of the poor, were the means to accomplish that end. This is where Saint Martin displayed that "energetic action and eager zeal to spread the faith" in a most heroic way. To Saint Martin, to be a doer was to become an apostle for Christ, the Christ who healed both bodies and souls.

Doers engaged in the apostolic life must possess the moral cardinal virtues, and this Saint Martin did to a most heroic degree. His self-control born of temperance was remarkable, wanting very little in the way of possessions, actually having no room of his own, eating sparsely of mostly sweet potatoes and water, wearing only the oldest, hand-me-down woolen habits, remaining chaste throughout his life.

His fortitude was truly remarkable. The highest act of fortitude is martyrdom, and he indicated willingness to experience it, having expressed hopes at one point of doing missionary work in Japan and in China. Although that was not God's plan for him, Martin displayed amazing fortitude throughout every one of the forty-five years he spent at the Dominican priory in Lima, willingly doing hard things for God and for the people around him. Just reading about his endless activities can be very tiring as well as inspiring! He was the barber for the Monastery of the Holy Rosary in Lima, nurse, surgeon, pharmacist, and indeed, veterinarian for the Dominicans and to the people of Lima, and all the while he was the guy who swept the floors and cleaned the toilets. There are also stories of marvelous endurance in feats such as single-handedly planting entire groves of trees.

Martin also embodied the practical wisdom of prudence as he crafted the means to reach his goals. He was definitely a man who got things done. He has been called the Father of Social Work. He raised vast sums of money and got money and goods to those who needed them most. He raised large numbers of dowries so young girls could get married, have families, and live fruitful, productive lives. It was estimated that he raised two thousand dollars per week from the rich to fund his various charitable causes, so confident were the benefactors in Martin's prudence in using those funds, the entirety of which would reach the intended recipients and fund the intended projects, including the establishment of hospitals, homes for the elderly, hospices for the terminally ill, and orphanages for abandoned poor children.

Another simple story of Martin's prudence, ingenuity, and respect for Dominican observances comes from a time when he was in charge of the priory's laundry. The friars had traditionally worn simple woolen habits, and Martin noticed that many of them had acquired or been given more elaborate and comfortable habits made of linen. For a time, when linen habits came in to be washed, he returned to the wearer a woolen habit of the same size. Never one to waste, and always one to show compassion for the sick, Martin kept the linen habits for use in the infirmary to make the sick more comfortable.

The last of the four cardinal virtues is justice, and great indeed was Saint Martin's love of justice. Indeed, the government of Peru, celebrating the three hundredth anniversary of his death on November 3, 1939, would declare him "the Patron and Special Protector of all works of Social Justice in Peru."[182] Justice renders to each person his rightful due, and Saint Martin believed all men and women had a right to learn the pathway to their salvation. Saint Martin also helped us come to learn what *every* person is rightfully due at a time when people were openly ranked and rated according to their race. I'll go into this more deeply as we consider the saint as a lover, but let me note something else here. Saint Thomas said that with justice we render to others what is their due, but in the virtue of *liberality*, we freely give them even more. Through justice we render people what is rightfully *theirs*; through liberality, we freely give them even from what is rightfully *our own*. Saint Martin lived and breathed the virtue of liberality, since he gave all he had, not in worldly possessions, since he had next to none to give, but he gave back to his neighbor through his good works all the invaluable spiritual gifts God had given him.

Saint Martin de Porres: Lover

The three theological virtues God infuses into our hearts and souls are, of course, faith, hope, and charity. There is no question of Saint Martin's deep Catholic faith and persevering hope in attaining salvation through God's aid, but the greatest of these God-given theological virtues is charity, or love, and it is here that we truly see Saint Martin in his greatest splendor. In my mind, he was a thinker and a doer indeed, but a lover par excellence.

[182] Richard Cardinal Cushing, *Saint Martin de Porres* (Boston: Daughters of Saint Paul, 1962), 56.

We have seen that Saint Thomas compared love to a furnace, and the more powerful the furnace, the farther will it warm with its heat. Martin strove to bring that love to the ends of the world. He sought to bring Christ to the Spanish, the aboriginal Andeans or Peruvians, to the Africans, and to all the mixed races in Peru. As was mentioned before, he also dreamed of doing missionary work in far-off countries such as Japan and China. Indeed, stories were told that God had given him the gift of bilocation, and he had mystically traveled to those places, as well as Africa and France. Some people who came to Lima said they spoke to him in those lands. He displayed medical knowledge known only in France at the time. Of this we can be sure: the furnace of Saint Martin's love reached around the world.

Indeed, the furnace of Saint Martin's love warmed not only men and women, but all sorts of animals too! There are numerous stories of Saint Martin's interventions, healing and feeding dogs, cats, mice, mules, cattle, chickens, et cetera. In one endearing story, he had a dog, a cat, and a mouse eating peacefully out of the same bowl. Although some people have considered this entertaining fair for the amusement and edification of children, some scholars have noted deeper levels of cultural and theological significance in these very numerous "little stories" people have told about Saint Martin. Some have noted, for example, that this story of the harmonious dog, cat, and mouse represents the harmony he sought to establish between the Spanish, the Indians, and the blacks of Peru.[183]

---

[183] See Alex Garcia-Rivera, *Saint Martin de Porres: The "Little Stories" and the Semiotics of Culture* (Maryknoll, NY: Orbis Books, 1995) for a fascinating analysis of many of these stories, and see Celia Cussen, *Black Saint of the Americas: The Life and Afterlife of Saint Martin de Porres* (New York: Cambridge University Press,

Another story relates that Martin would arise before 4:30 each morning to fulfill his duties as his priory's *campanero*, that is, bell-ringer. Well, early in the morning, a cat would work its way into Martin's cell and pull on his habit until Martin woke up. The most interesting tidbit is in the details, since the cat was said to be white, black, and brown, a *mestizo*, of mixed breed, like Martin himself. Does this story not convey a powerful message about the man who would ring the bell to draw the white, black, and brown together to sing harmonious praises to their common Father?

Martin brought people together in his time and does so even in ours, and that phenomenon was seen clearly at his canonization proceedings. Thousands of people from dozens of nations gathered together at the Vatican on May 6, 1962, including 3,000 from Spain, 1,000 from Peru, 350 African-Americans (and half of them Protestant!), and 1,500 from Ireland,[184] and that Irish contingent brings an illuminating parallel to mind.

My first exemplar in writing of a loving saint of "the charitable style" was Saint Brigid of Ireland (ca. 453–525).[185] She, like Saint Martin, was and still is well known and loved for her compassion and acts of mercy for the sick and the poor, along with unmatched sweetness, kindness, and liberal hospitality. And here is the fascinating parallel. A legend relates that it was prophesied that Saint Brigid would be born neither outside nor inside and that she would bring great good to the world. As the story goes, she was born while her mother, carrying a pail of milk, was crossing the threshold into her house, neither completely

---

2014) for a recent and very thorough account of the story of Saint Martin's life and the canonization process and testimonies.

[184] Cushing, 12, 48.

[185] Kevin Vost, *Three Irish Saints: A Guide to Finding Your Spiritual Style* (Charlotte, NC: TAN Books, 2012).

outside nor inside! But could this amusing Irish "little story" have a deeper significance with a lesson much like that of the life of Saint Martin de Porres? Well, Saint Brigid's father was a powerful Irish chieftain, and her mother was his unmarried slave. Does that ring any bells regarding our Spanish-African bell-ringer?

Some argue with good reason that part of Saint Brigid's success was due to the fact that she could relate to those of both worlds, both the rich and the poor, the powerful and the oppressed, and this too was true of Martin. Although he did not fit in completely with the Spanish, African, or native Peruvians around him, in another important sense, he had ties with and could relate to them all. His heart and compassion went out to care for African slaves, poor native Peruvians, and also rich Spaniards who sought him out for healing or for spiritual counsel. Martin referred to Africans and native Peruvians as *hijos* (my children), and his closest friend and spiritual son in the last years of his life was a Spaniard with the same first name as his father, known now as Saint Juan Macias, O.P.

One compelling little story shows Martin's compassion for animals and for African slaves, and his lack of contempt for some uncharitable brothers. Once at a Dominican farm outside Lima, where Saint Martin would work planting herbs and trees and while visiting native and African farmworkers, some friars came across Martin late at night feeding mules and oxen. His brother friars chided him and told him to leave work like that for the Africans. Martin did not lash out at them for their lack of charity. He simply answered that the Africans were tired and even the animals had worked harder than he had that day. Indeed, he said he had done nothing to serve God that day and didn't want the day to pass without some kind of service. Hopefully those friars learned from his humble response and his tender loving action more than they would have learned from a rebuke.

Any animal lover will cherish the many stories of Saint Martin's tender loving care of the little creatures of God, because he never forgot that that is what they are. All kinds of species were recipients of his care, but perhaps the stars of most of these stories are dogs. Indeed, at one point Marin was ordered to clear out the veritable dog hospital he had established at the priory, so he moved them to the house of his sister. So great was his love for God's creatures that some have called Saint Martin the Saint Francis of the Americas (as one author notes — no small feat for a Dominican!).

And speaking of dogs, Saint Martin was clearly a most unique breed of hound of the Lord. In fact, in a time of great racial prejudice and discrimination, the dark-skinned, biracial Martin was often referred to as a mulatto dog, even at times by his brother friars. Recalling how Saint Catherine emphasized that contrary vices can prove and develop virtues, we see this in action in the way such treatment actually flamed the fires of forgiveness, humility, and charity within Saint Martin's heart.

When people would taunt him by calling him a mulatto dog, Martin did not fight back, or merely shrug it off, but often sought these people out to do good works for them. When his friends would reprove him for this, he would say, "These people truly know me." In the most poignant example, he was nursing an older ailing priest scheduled to have his leg amputated the next day. The priest started berating him and called him a mulatto dog, perhaps envying Martin's youth, his joy, or his health. A witness said Martin chuckled to himself as he left the room. He discerned that the priest had been craving a salad seasoned with capers.[186] He came back the next day and served the priest such a salad. The priest savored his meal, begged Brother Martin's

---

[186] *Capparis spinosa*, whose flowerbuds are used as a tasty seasoning.

forgiveness, and indeed, his leg was healed. Would that we all could repay insults with such savory capers of kindness!

Throughout his sixty years of life, Saint Martin displayed that tender kindness that reveals the heart of the charitable lover. Biographer Giuliana Cavallini waxes euphoric in three paragraphs merely about Martin's smile. She notes that virtually all who gave a deposition for his canonization had something to say about his loving smile. In her words:

> Martin's smile was veiled with sorrow by the sorrow of others, but when he himself was suffering it was more luminous than ever. It was a constant smile, not a fixed one. The purity and ardor of his soul were revealed by it, and in his contacts with others it had nuances of inexpressible delicacy, as light takes on indefinable tones and shades of color from the objects on which it falls. His smile gave courage to the timid, comfort to sufferers, confidence to those who faltered, hope to the oppressed. Most important of all, it always aroused distaste for evil and love of good.[187]

Perhaps we all should pray for a smile like Saint Martin's and build up our facial and spiritual muscles by sharing it with everyone.

The Death and Ongoing Life of a Saint Who Can Bring Us Together

In the last months of his life, Saint Martin contracted a fatal illness (most likely typhus) from which he told others he knew there was no cure. He was well treated by his fellow Dominican

---

[187] Giuliana Cavallini, *Saint Martin de Porres: Apostle of Charity* (Rockford, IL: TAN Books, 2000), 44–45.

brothers but hesitated to change out of the simple woolen habit of the donado that he had chosen to wear even as a religious brother. He refused offers of medicines that would be procured by the killing of animals. When he died surrounded by the presence and prayers of his brother friars on November 3, 1639, it was a time of great lamentation for all of Lima. Proceedings for his eventual beatification and canonization got under way very soon, but for a variety of reasons and events (including the sinking in a storm of a ship carrying deposition documents from Peru to the Vatican), Martin was not declared a blessed until 1837, not long before the American Civil War, which resulted in the emancipation of slaves, and was not canonized until 1962, at the time of the great civil rights movement spearheaded by another Christian leader of African descent who bore the name of Martin.

Biographer Sister Mary Alphonsus, O.S.S.R., relates that Martin's lineage on his father's side can be traced back to a fifth-century ancestor who gained famed in fighting with the Frankish King Clovis in a war against the Moors. Martin's ancestor felled the Moorish king with a cudgel[188] and proudly took *cudgel* as the family name. (In Spanish, *cudgel* is *porras*.) We read in Scripture of the time to come when people will "beat their swords into plowshares" (Isa. 2:4). How amazing that through God's grace Saint Martin turned his family cudgel of war into a broom of peace. May we all learn from Saint Martin the lessons of love, harmony, and unity that all the world so desperately needs right now in the eight hundredth Jubilee of the order this saint called his own.

---

[188] A short, thick club or bludgeon used in battle. Sister's biographical novel is *Saint Martin de Porres: A Dramatic Story* (New York: Saint Martin de Porres Guild, 1966).

Saint Catherine de Ricci

1522–1589 | FEAST: FEBRUARY 13

Although few of us today actively seek out intense, protracted suffering to chastise our flesh and liberate our souls, at some point or another, virtually every one of us is going to endure some suffering, either our own or that of someone we love. The lessons of saints who particularly embraced Christ's suffering are lessons we would be wise not to ignore. We saw the trials and mortifications of Saint Catherine of Siena, and soon we'll become familiar with the many crosses that Saint Rose of Lima freely chose to bear. Saint Catherine de Ricci is another great Dominican saint who can teach us how God's love can conquer all suffering.

Alexandra de Ricci was born of noble stock in Prato, near Florence, Italy. Her mother died when she was young, and Alexandra turned to the Blessed Mother for love and solace. As a child, she was sent to a monastery of which her aunt was the abbess, and there she developed such a devotion to Christ's Passion that a crucifix at which she would kneel and pray enrapt is still called "Alexandra's crucifix." At thirteen, she would enter a Dominican convent at which her uncle was the confessor. She took the name of Catherine and would eventually become the prioress.

Saint Catherine was best known for a most unusual mystical experience. Starting at the age of twenty, for a period of twelve years, on every Thursday from noon until 4:00 p.m. on Friday, she would miraculously experience the "ecstasy of the Passion," feeling the experience of Christ's sufferings in his last hours, and receiving the stigmata. Her fellow sisters could discern the course of the Passion from the look on her face, as she was mystically scourged, crowned with thorns, et cetera. The next time we pray the Stations of the Cross we might do well to recall Catherine's holy passion for the Passion.

Saint Rose of Lima and the Fragrant Love Born of Suffering

*As thorns spring forth with roses, so grief and pain seem
to have been born with the blessed Rose; for her life was a
tissue of sufferings, sickness, pains, and crosses, which
exercised her patience from her cradle to her tomb,
by a long and tedious martyrdom.*
—Fr. Jean Baptist Feuillet, O.P.,
The Life of Saint Rose of Lima

*And after you have suffered a little while, the God of all
grace, who has called you to his eternal glory in Christ,
will himself restore, establish, and strengthen you.*
—1 Peter 5:10

A Saint You Can Always Bank On

We have seen how the life of a man of mixed race from almost four hundred years ago and a continent away has so many lessons to teach and examples to follow in sharing God's love in our lives today. Saint Martin de Porres, the "mulatto dog" of the

Lord, did so many ordinary things in the most extraordinary ways. Within the span of Saint Martin's life, and within the confines of his city, we find another astounding saint and loving hound of the Lord, and yet, at a superficial level, her life and her lessons may seem very odd, extreme, and strange to us today. Although known for her surpassing beauty and her childlike heart, she is perhaps known best for self-inflicted penitential suffering and self-mortification hardly surpassed in the life of any saint, and an earthly death at merely thirty-one years of age.

Are there lessons those of us, perhaps so much older, and so many centuries later, can learn from the gruesome crosses that she chose to bear? Does the life of Saint Rose of Lima have relevance today?

I say yes, you can bank on it. Perhaps the most surprising place we can see an unmistakable sign that this young virgin saint still touches people's lives in the most popular and positive of ways is the fact the nation of Peru honors her as we do Benjamin Franklin. That unmistakable sign is the dollar sign, so to speak. Benjamin Franklin (1706–1790) is honored by his depiction on the United States' highest denomination of currency in circulation, the hundred-dollar bill. Saint Rose of Lima (1586–1617) is honored by her depiction on Peru's highest denomination of currency in circulation, the 200 *nuevos soles* banknote. The saying "A penny saved is a penny earned" is often attributed to Franklin. To Saint Rose a penny given away to meet the needs of the poor was a penny best spent, for the sign she truly stood for was not the dollar sign but the sign of the Cross of her Savior.

Let's look at a thumbnail sketch of her youth (complete with an actual thumbnail story) before we consider the most holy ways this beloved daughter of Saint Dominic lived the contemplative, apostolic, and charitable life as a thinker, doer, and lover for Christ.

Thumbnail Sketch of the Youth of Saint Rose

Rose was born on April 20, 1586, in Lima, Peru, but miles from Saint Martin de Porres, when he was a boy of seven. Her father, Gaspar de Flores,[189] was a Spaniard employed by the Spanish army, and her mother, Maria de Oliva, was a Creole of Spanish and native Peruvian-Indian heritage. Rose, their eleventh child, was named Isabel after her aunt and godmother but soon acquired the lasting nickname of Rose when their servant Mariana reported a mystical vision of her face transformed into a rose one day as she rested in her crib. Years later, in 1597, when she was confirmed by Saint Turibius Mongrovejo, the same man who confirmed Saint Martin de Porres, he reportedly called her Rose, which she then took as her lasting name.

Rose's suffering and her unusual capacity to bear pain are presented in stories from her first years of life. The aforementioned thumbnail incident occurred when she was three. Her thumb was severely smashed in an accident, but Rose acted as if nothing happened and did not tell her family. Her mother noticed later when the thumb had become horribly infected and required surgical intervention. Rose did not scream or even change her facial expression when the surgeon had to rip out the nail from its roots. Not long later, she bore it just as placidly when the surgeon had to remove part of her ear that had been badly infected — these operations, of course, done without anesthetics. When asked if it hurt, she replied that it hurt a little, but the Lord's crown of thorns must have hurt much more.

[189] "Of the flowers."

Rose was also subjected to emotional sufferings during the years of her childhood, as her hot-tempered mother would coddle and pamper her sometimes and severely punish her at other times. She was well aware of Rose's unusual beauty and dreamed of marrying her into a rich and respected family someday.[190] Rose, however, from the earliest age, had little concern for the things of the world. A story relates that one day when she was five and was out playing with other children, one of them threw dirt in her hair, and when she became upset, her brother Fernando told her not to be upset, saying something to the effect that she should not be angry because concern with fine hair is a vanity, and men's hearts become bound by a girl's pretty hair and can be drawn thereby into hell. Her brother's advice may seem a bit drastic to some ears, but it is reported that from this time on, Rose swore off the vanities of the world, devoted herself to Christ, and patterned her life after what she had learned of the life of Saint Catherine of Siena.

Like Saint Catherine, Rose embarked on a life filled with prayer, fasting, and self-mortifications, which will be detailed later. Although her parents were clearly aware of Rose's piety and devotions, like Saint Catherine, for many years she did not tell them of the vow of virginity she had made as a child. Her mother would continue to dress her lavishly, take her to parties

---

[190] Just as I completed the text of this book, modern forensic scientists, using her skull preserved by the Dominicans, completed a hypothetical reconstruction of the beautiful face of Saint Rose. For a look at her stunning face and the intriguing story behind the project see "Is This What Saint Rose of Lima Looked Like?" Catholic News Agency, August 28, 2015, accessed September 26, 2015, http://www.catholicnewsagency.com/news/is-this-what-saint-rose-of-lima-looked-like-43764/.

and other social visits as she schemed to arrange a husband for her. Many young men were willing to court the beautiful Rose, but she so opposed this that at times she would rub pepper over her face and eyes to render her face less beautiful. Even after age twenty, when Rose donned the Dominican habit of the Third Order, as had Saint Catherine before her, her mother had hoped that she would still marry, as members of the Third Order were not cloistered, did not take religious vows, and were free to marry if they chose to do so.

Rose's late childhood and teenage years were spent immersed in prayer and chores within her family's household and outside in their small garden. Rose's family was large and poor. In addition to regular household chores, she became quite expert in needlework and in embroidering silks, and so beautiful were the intricate floral designs she produced that some said she was helped by angels. Here we see why Rose would become a patron saint of embroiderers, and those who had seen the family garden tended and the bouquets that she arranged would not be at all surprised to see she would one day become a saintly patroness for gardeners too. *Ora et labora*, "pray and work," the ancient motto of the monasteries, nearly sums up Rose's entire youth.

Around the age of twenty, Rose felt the calling to a deeper commitment to Christ and desired to join a religious order. Archbishop Turibius himself requested that Rose join a convent of Poor Clares, newly founded by his niece. The Augustinian Convent of the Incarnation also actively sought Rose out, and she apparently decided to join them. When she went to the Dominican Chapel of the Rosary and knelt down in prayer to bid the Blessed Virgin farewell, she found herself unable to rise, even with the help of her brother. She decided to return home instead of the convent and found herself able to stand up and go.

Rose believed this was a sign from heaven, and she soon received a second sign as clear as day in black and white. Soon after in her garden, amid a sea of flowers and multicolored butterflies, a black and white butterfly, having the colors of the Dominican habit, came and fluttered around her heart, leaving a mark on her dress in the shape of a heart. This confirmed in Rose's mind and heart her intention to follow in the footsteps of Saint Catherine and join the Third Order Dominicans.

For the next eleven years of her life, Saint Rose wore the habit and lived a life of penance, prayer, and good works for the sick and the poor, living most of the time in a very small hermitage she and her brother Fernando built back in the family garden. How she prayed there, what she did when she ventured out in the world, and how it all was inspired by and overflowed into love are what we'll consider next.

Thinker: The Mystic Rose of Lima

Saint Rose, like Saint Martin, was clearly no philosopher or theologian like Saints Albert and Thomas, yet every saint, and indeed every one of us, has been given an intellect and instructed by Christ to love God with all our heart, soul, *and mind* (cf. Matt. 22:37). Every Dominican too, as we have seen again and again, is especially called to share with others the fruits of his *contemplation*. Rose was not an academic and had little in the way of formal education, although she did learn to read. Among her favorite books were biographies of Saint Catherine of Siena and the spiritual guidebooks of another notable Dominican, Venerable Louis of Granada.[191] In fact, his *Book of Prayer and Meditation* became Saint Rose's favorite book, as prayer and meditation themselves were

[191] Whom we met earlier in More Hounds of the Lord.

to become her favorite activities, forming the core and shaping the periphery of every aspect of her short life.

Rose's life of prayer and contemplation started very early from the time of her early childhood when she would find herself drawn to stare at a picture of Christ crowned in thorns. She also had a special devotion to the Child Jesus and to his Blessed Mother. Saints drawn to prayer and contemplation seek to follow Christ's instruction to "go into your room and shut the door and pray to your Father who is in secret" (Matt. 6:6). They seek communion with the Father and not the eyes and the praise of others. When circumstances allow it, some go out into the desert, up into the mountains, or within some densely wooded glen. Others, like Saints Catherine and Rose, must seek their sanctuary of prayer, exactly as Christ explained it, from within the confines of their room.

Much of Rose's prayer in her adult life would take place throughout the night in her little hermitage outside in the garden. As an early biographer puts it, her family would tell visitors, "If you wish to find Rose, you must look for her in her garden; that is her bedroom, her table, and her oratory; she never leaves it."[192] This little wooden room she shut herself in was merely five feet long by four feet wide, hardly more than a modern standard closet. When people were astonished by its small size, Rose would say there was plenty of room for Jesus and her! Here she would pray throughout the night, fighting against sleep so diligently that at times she would tie a length of her hair to a peg on the wall behind her so that she would be awakened if she nodded off during prayer.

---

[192] Frederick William Faber, *The Life of Saint Rose of Lima* (Philadelphia: Peter F. Cunningham and Son, 1855), 77.

Enclosed in her private hermitage, Rose read books on meditative prayer, especially, as mentioned, those of Venerable Louis of Granada. She devoutly prayed the Rosary and used many other vocal and mental forms of prayer. She would meditate for hours simply on the multitude of graces she had received through God's mercy. She also asked her confessor to compile a list of 150 perfections of God, and one of her favorite prayers would come to involve hours-long meditations on God's justice, mercy, omnipotence, wisdom, et cetera. Rose said that this kind of prayer was pleasing to God and hateful to the devils that sometimes tormented her.

Christ said of those who pray to the Father in secret that "your Father who sees in secret will reward you" (Matt. 6:6), and Saint Rose was rewarded with many ecstatic visions, including, like Saint Catherine, a divine espousal with Christ.

Doer: The Rose Takes Up Her Cross

Rose was not a doer in the grand sense of a Saint Dominic, who founded an order, or Saint Catherine, who influenced popes, although she was admired by her saintly archbishop, and Lima once credited her with saving the city through her prayers. Lima was on the brink of destruction by a squadron of Dutch pirates, who turned around and sailed away after Rose had gone to the church to pray and to defend the altar. Most of what Rose did was done on a smaller, although most arduous scale. She knew well that Christ has said that those who would follow Him will need to deny themselves daily and take up their cross (Matt. 16:24; Luke 9:23). These are hard words of holy advice that she heeded like few before her or since.

Saint Thomas wrote that the cardinal virtues of temperance, fortitude, justice, and prudence pertain to the active life, but they also prepare us to rein in our passions and focus our intellect and will so that we might rise undisturbed to the heights of contemplation. Saint Rose displayed those cardinal virtues in the most heroic degree, and she is probably best known for her unusual degree of both temperance and fortitude as displayed in the many extreme and most difficult ways she contrived to take up Christ's cross through her own daily (and nightly) acts of self-denial and self-mortification.

Temperance reins in our sensual desires for bodily pleasures, and few pulled in their reins tighter than young Rose. As for the senses of the palate, she gave up meat as a child, as well as the succulent fruits of the tropical clime of Peru. She would often deprive herself of cold water, and of any water at all, and would live on things such as bread crusts and simple bitter herbs. As for the sensual pleasures of the body, although Rose would at times be tormented by visions of temptations toward vanity and toward bodily pleasures, through God's grace she never consented to such sins and persevered in her vows of chastity and purity.

Fortitude calls forth our "irascible" powers, whereby we hate evil things and fire up our courage to overcome evil obstacles to obtain difficult goods, even if those obstacles should threaten our life and limb. Christian fortitude is the God-given ability to do hard things for the honor and glory of God. It is the power to take up those crosses Christ told us about. This, of all virtues, but for the love of *charity*, was perhaps the strongest of all within the sturdy soul of this ostensibly delicate Rose. She hated the thought of any demon, any sensation, any wicked thought or intention that might stir her will against the will of God, and in her personal war against any possible vice or sin, she devised self-mortifications that may well boggle the modern mind, and prompted some of her own confessors to command her to tone some of them down.

To provide but a few examples of Saint Rose's self-imposed penances and mortifications, she so fought against sleep that would deprive her of time for prayer that she devised a bed for herself that was a little wooden box with a mattress stuffed with hard, gnarled pieces of wood and broken pottery chards that allowed for but a few hours of sleep when she was very tired. She devised a veil of thorns of sorts, a band full of sharp points on the inside that she could tighten with a string that was attached. Her family discovered this when her father once accidentally struck her on the head as she got between him and a brother, and the family saw little streams of blood pour down her face. When she told the incident to her confessor, he had the sharp points filed down. At times in her garden, she would literally take up a heavy wooden cross, in imitation of Christ's Passion. Even as a child, it was said that she asked their servant Mariana to mistreat her, spit on her, and load her back with heavy stones and logs until she fell under their weight. As an adult she would rinse her mouth with bitter sheep's gall. She also disciplined herself with an iron chain, until her confessor forbade it. She then bound the chain tightly around her waist and threw away the key.

Saint Rose's mortifications may seem very strange to us today, but they still may hold valuable lessons. In Saint Dominic's "third way of prayer," he employed the discipline of striking himself with an iron chain while repeating (translated) from the Latin Vulgate Bible "Your discipline has set me straight towards my goal" (Psalm 17:36). Physical spiritual disciplines were not unusual in Rose's time, although she practiced them to an unusual degree. Some today might wonder if Rose's self-mortifications were a sign of scrupulosity or mental instability, and this was also considered in her time. Due to the unusual manner of her penitential life, Rose was once questioned by several theologians and a medical doctor of the Inquisition, but these learned men concluded that hers was a life unusually graced by God.

The use of pepper to disfigure her eyes and her face and the piercing of her skin with the little silver nails of her crown or with the ceramic shards in her bed may suggest to some of us today a masochism or perhaps a desperate call for attention, but we'd be wise to consider what motivated such acts and to compare and contrast them with some very popular modern practices. We need only look around us today to see the millions of young people who pay to have their skin penetrated by needles so that they may be injected with dyes or perforated to hold metal ornaments. These acts are performed so that attention will be drawn to the bearer of those tattoos and piercings, their clear message being, "Look at me!" When Rose peppered her face or pierced the skin of her forehead or back, she did so in secret, sometimes explicitly so that others would *not* look at her, as was the case with the pepper, but most often by far so that she could forget the cares of the world and better look at Christ.

Although we may not be called to such extreme acts of conquering our wills, can we not still learn something from them? Can they inspire us to pamper our own bodies a little less, to mortify our sensual desires a little more, so that our thoughts can rise to higher things? Even the noble pagan philosophers saw the need for self-discipline in order to acquire virtue. The Stoic Epictetus, for example, encouraged such simple acts. He encouraged those who would love wisdom to discipline their bodies, not by "hugging statues," an action some Cynics would perform while bare-chested in the winter's cold — public statues, of course, so that others might see them. In advice prescient in some ways of one of Saint Rose's little disciplines some fourteen hundred years later, Epictetus suggested instead to fill one's mouth with water when thirsty, but then to spit it out—when no one is looking. (The Father, of course, knows what we do in secret.)

Justice means rendering to each person his due, and this Rose always rendered, and then some. In the last years of her life, Rose persuaded her mother to allow her to care for the poor, the homeless, the elderly, and the sick in empty rooms of their house, and her actions are considered, along with those of Saint Martin de Porres, among the foundations of social work in Peru.

Prudence is that practical wisdom that finds the right means to get things done, and in this virtue Rose also shined. We see her prudence in the way she was always able to incorporate deeds of the active life while immersed in a life of solitude, prayer, and contemplation, as she prayed while she cleaned, embroidered, gardened, and made and sold flower arrangements. We saw it toward the end of her life when, failing in health and deep in contemplation, she made those practical arrangements to tend to the bodily and spiritual needs of those who needed them the most.

Lover: Christ's Yoke of Charity Is Light

Rose never failed to carry her cross, but she never forgot that He who called us to carry it and follow Him also declared that if we come to him, He will give us rest to our souls, "For my yoke is easy, and my burden light" (Matt. 11:30). At the bidding of Saint Bernard of Clairvaux (1090–1153), Cistercian friar Saint Aelred of Rievaulx (1110–1167) wrote a book called *The Mirror of Charity*, in which he made clear in such eloquent words that "this yoke does not oppress but unites; this burden has wings, not weight.

This yoke is charity. This burden is brotherly love."[193] Those who complain about the weight of Christ's burden are those who have weighed themselves down with worldly concerns instead. As all virtues lead us on toward Christ, "like a carriage for someone weary, food for the wayfarer's journey, a lamp for those groping in darkness, weapons for those waging battle," it is charity that provides "rest for the weary, an inn for the wayfarer, full light at the journey's end, and the perfect crown for the victor."[194]

Although our sixteenth-century Peruvian Dominican was unlikely to have read the works of this twelfth-century English Cistercian, she clearly reflected those lessons of charity in the mirror of her heart.

Rose's penances and manifold virtues were merely the means that sought out the ends of charity, to love of God with all one's heart, soul, and strength, and one's neighbor as oneself.

This great love for God was seen most clearly in Rose's devotion to the Eucharist. She sought to receive Communion daily, and upon reception of our Lord, she would remain in a state of prayerful ecstasy for hours. When Rose sought out martyrdom with the pirates at Lima's shores, she had run to the altar to give her life if necessary to prevent the desecration of the Blessed Sacrament.

Knowing well the lessons of her model and comfort, Saint Catherine of Siena, Saint Rose knew that God gave us each other as instruments through which to display and grow in our love for Him. We have seen the tender, loving care Rose provided for the physical needs of poor, the sick, orphans, and the

---

[193] Aelred of Rievaulx, *The Mirror of Charity* (Kalamazoo, MI: Cistercian Publications, 1990), 133.
[194] Ibid., 140–141.

elderly, but like her spiritual father, Saint Dominic, this hound
of the Lord was also quite hungry for souls to bring back to the
Father. Her many corporal works of mercy were always accompanied by a host of spiritual works of mercy too.[195]

As gentle, loving, and reserved as she was, she did not hesitate to do things like "reprove the sinner" even with nobles
and even in Church, for she was known to chastise people who
disrespectfully carried on conversations out loud during Mass.

So great was her zeal for God and her desire to bring souls
to Him that she frequently prayed for the conversion of the
native Indian people who lived in the mountains, and she did
what she could to encourage those who would go and preach to
them. In fact, one time she emboldened a reticent missionary by
promising him half of all the spiritual merits she had earned if he
would go out to evangelize them. Rose's love, like Saint Martin's,
knew no bounds of class, ethnicity, or nationality. She cared for
rich and poor, for the Spanish, the Indians, and the Africans,
and she talked about dreams of a mission to Japan, welcoming
the chance to be martyred there for Christ.[196]

---

[195] Saint Thomas Aquinas lists the traditional seven Corporal
Works of Mercy as feeding the hungry, giving drink to the thirsty,
clothing the naked, harboring the homeless, visiting the sick,
ransoming captives, and burying the dead; and the seven Spiritual Works of Mercy as instructing the ignorant, counseling
the doubtful, comforting the sorrowful, reproving the sinner,
forgiving injuries, bearing wrongs patiently, and praying for the
living and the dead. He wrote that these works of mercy are at
their core "act[s] of charity through the medium of mercy." *ST*,
II-II, Q. 32, art. 1.

[196] Around Saint Rose's time, hundreds of Catholic missionaries
would be martyred there. Among the most famous Dominican
martyrs was Blessed Alphonsus Naverette, who, in 1617 (the
year Saint Rose died) traveled with an Augustinian companion

Rose's Last Days on Earth and First Years in Heaven

At a mere thirty-one years of age, on the night of July 31, Rose's last days of terminal illness began as she was assailed by fevers and a variety of ailments, including pneumonia, asthma, rheumatism, and gout. She suffered and ached in virtually every muscle, bone, and organ, and yet she remained serene and uncomplaining. On August 23, the eve of the feast of the apostle Saint Bartholomew, she requested blessings from her family and friends who surrounded her. Near midnight she said that she heard a mysterious noise that announced her Divine Spouse was coming to meet her. She asked her brother to remove the mattress underneath her and the pillow from behind her head, so that she, like Christ, might die upon pieces of wood. Twice she exclaimed, "Jesus, be with me!" and then her soul was with Him. Rose died on earth and rose in heaven on August 24, 1617.

The fragrant love that rose from Rose's suffering was recognized in all of Lima and throughout Peru. Her funeral was vast and well attended by the people and by all of the city's public officials. Very soon the process toward her canonization was under way, complete with more than 180 depositions regarding her sanctity, and the miraculous healing effects of her clothing, her pictures, and even the earth in which she had been buried. Fifty years after her death, in 1667 she would be beatified by Pope Clement IX, and four years later, in 1671, she would be canonized by his successor, Pope Clement X. She would be declared a patroness of Latin America and of the Philippines as well.

---

to Omura to obtain the relics of two martyred priests, a Franciscan and a Jesuit. Along the way they were captured, tortured, and martyred by beheading.

To end with a note on the personal scale, it seems that Rose's mother never really understood her daughter throughout her short life on earth. Maria loved her Rose but often presented obstacles to her, for the path she had in mind for Rose was not the path that Christ had paved. Rose loved her mother none the less for the hardships she put on her, for she considered all trials gifts from God to test her love for Him and to foster her growth in virtue. Rose had prophesied while alive that a Dominican Convent of Saint Catherine of Siena would be completed in Lima and that her mother would join it. The convent was completed, and after Gaspar's death, Maria did take those vows, growing to appreciate better Rose's special calling and becoming, like her daughter, a daughter of Christ and a hound of the Lord in the Order of Saint Dominic.

Saint Louis Marie Grignon de Montfort

1673–1716 | FEAST: APRIL 28

From Saint Dominic on, the hounds of the Lord have always been especially loyal to the Blessed Mother of God. It was said that the Virgin Mary provided Blessed Reginald of Orléans and Saint Dominic himself with the distinctive Dominican scapular. Saint Dominic and the early Dominicans were also early champions of the holy Rosary. As we saw earlier, Pope Saint Pius V would establish October 7 as the Feast of Our Lady of the Rosary, attributing the Christian success at the Battle of Lepanto to her intercession. There is yet another hound of the Lord who literally wrote the book on true devotion to the Blessed Virgin, ever so aptly entitled *True Devotion to Mary*.[197]

Born in Montfort in north-central France, Louis was trained by Jesuits and Sulpicians and became a diocesan priest. He joined the Third Order of Saint Dominic and traveled throughout Europe fostering Marian devotion through the Rosary. Three centuries later, Pope Saint John Paul II would tell the world that after reading de Montfort's life-changing *True Devotion*, it was "from Montfort that I have taken my motto: 'Totus tuus' [I am all thine (Mary)]."

[197] His other Marian works are *The Secret of Mary* and *The Secret of the Rosary*.

It is unfortunate that some of our non-Catholic Christian brothers and sisters do not realize the blessings that come from honoring her who prophesied "all generations will call me blessed" (Luke 1:48). (If only they would heed the barking of the hounds of the Lord!) Saint Louis Marie Grignon de Montfort, a man who took that blessed handmaid's name as part of his own, understood those blessings so well, as he summed up in his own words: "If we are establishing devotion to our Blessed Lady, it is only in order to establish devotion to our Lord more perfectly."

Blessed Pier Giorgio Frassati Ascends to the Heights of Love

Born in Heaven on the Fourth of July

On July 4, 1776, fifty-six men signed a revolutionary declaration that included the powerful statement "that all men are created

equal, that they are endowed by their Creator with certain un-
alienable Rights, that among these are Life, Liberty and the
pursuit of Happiness." These men and their fellow citizens would
later found a nation with a constitution including a bill of rights
containing ten amendments, the first words of the First Amend-
ment being: "Congress shall make no law respecting an establishment of religion, or prohibiting the free exercise thereof."[198]
One signer of that Declaration of Independence, and the second
president of the United States that it gave birth to, would later
write: "Our Constitution was made only for a moral and religious
people. It is wholly inadequate to the government of any other."

On July 4, 1826, fifty years to the day after that declaration
was signed, that man, ninety-year-old John Adams, lay suffering
on his deathbed while the nation he helped to found raucously
celebrated its fiftieth Independence Day. His last reported words
referred to the only other surviving member of the original group
of American revolutionaries: "Thomas Jefferson still lives!"

Thomas Jefferson had not only signed, but at a mere thirty-
three years of age, had written that declaration defending and
celebrating the rights of life, liberty, and happiness bestowed on
us by our Creator. He would also later lead the nation it birthed,
following Adams as the third U.S. president. When Adams had
declared his last words regarding this dear friend of the last years
of their lives, he was unaware that five hours before, on that same
Fourth of July, Jefferson too, at age eighty-two, had passed on to
meet their Creator.

On July 4, 1925, ninety-nine years later, and 4,100 miles
across the Atlantic in the city of Turin, Italy, another defender
of God-given freedom lay in his deathbed at a mere twenty-four

---

[198] The Bill of Rights was ratified on December 15, 1791.

years of age. He had fought not against King George and the oppressive British monarchy, but against Benito Mussolini and the fast-rising and brutal Fascist Party. He was a political activist and staunch public defender of faith but was known even more for his tender acts of loving care to the poorest and the sickest who needed it most. His speeches and writings would include sentiments like these: "When we all accept Christ's voice and teaching, we will be able to say we are equal and every difference between human beings will be annulled,"[199] and "Through charity, peace is sown among people, not the peace that the world gives but the true peace that only faith in Christ can give us, making us brothers and sisters."[200] His last words would be to ask his family to be sure to check his coat so they could deliver some medicines he had in one pocket to a sick man in need, and in another, a pawn ticket he had obtained to help another poor friend reclaim a precious item he had pawned in order to eat. That young man was Pier Giorgio Frassati.

This young martyr, in a sense, to the causes of social justice and loving interpersonal charity, worked so humbly and without self-promotion or fanfare that his mother and his father, who was a senator, an ambassador, and the owner and editor of a prominent newspaper, were astounded when they saw the massive public reaction to the death of their young son, a young man who had not yet completed his schooling and embarked on a career, and indeed, a son they had considered to be a bit of a dullard.

---

[199] Luciana Frassati, *A Man of the Beatitudes: Pier Giorgio Frassati* (San Francisco: Ignatius Press, 2001), 57.

[200] Ibid., 170–171, from Pope Saint John Paul II's April 24, 1984, address to eighty thousand youths at the Olympic Stadium in Rome during the International Jubilee for Athletes.

We saw that Saint Thomas Aquinas explained how great teachers are like mountains that, watered by the rains of God's wisdom, pass down their life-giving streams to all the valleys of the earth below them. Pier Giorgio Frassati loved to contemplate God from actual mountain peaks and then to come down and pass on to others the succulent fruits of his joyous contemplations. He was a most loyal hound of the Lord, and all of us can learn volumes on living a life of love in Christ if we would but hear the bark of his preaching still echoing loudly from the heights of the mountaintops even in our day.

The Life in Brief of the Brief Life of Pier Giorgio Frassati

On April 6, 1901, on a Holy Saturday in the city of Turin, Italy, Alfredo Frassati and his wife, Adelaide Ametis, named their first-born son Pier Giorgio. Alfredo was an agnostic, and Adelaide went to Mass but did not go to Communion or kneel to pray, and yet, like his first namesake, their son would always stand fast in defense of the Church, and like his second namesake, he would one day bravely battle with dragons.[201] Seventeen months later, the couple would give birth to Luciana, Pier Giorgio's most cherished lifelong companion, and in his afterlife, his biographer and champion.

The children spent much of their time in their early years at the estate of their devout grandmother Linda Ametis. Their father, engrossed in his work as founder, owner, and editor-in-chief of the influential newspaper *La Stampa*,[202] and later as the

---

[201] Peter George in Anglicized form. His "dragons" wore the black shirts of Italy's Fascist militia.

[202] *La Stampa*, "the Press," is still published today.

youngest Italian senator and the ambassador to Germany, had little time to devote to his children's daily lives. Luciana reports that he only asked of his children: "Love each other. Do not play cards. Study."[203] Now, the first and the last of these requests sure sound Dominican to me! The second is not so much so, since while Dominic advised his sons and daughters to embrace poverty, Alfredo's prohibition of card playing expressed his great worry that his son and daughter would embrace poverty, squandering the family fortune that he had amassed!

Their mother, Adelaide, was a socially connected woman of influence, immersed in affairs of the world and with special interest and talent in painting. Indeed, one of her works of art was purchased and displayed by the King of Italy, Emmanuel III. Both parents prohibited their children from playing with other children when they were little, and Pier Giorgio and Luciana grew very close, despite their different personalities and interests. Luciana later succinctly summed up one difference: "I liked success; he liked poverty."[204]

From his earliest years, despite a lack of formal training in the Catholic Faith, Pier Giorgio's selfless acts of Christian kindness and hospitality abounded, and a small sample of these will be told in our section about him as a "lover." Pier Giorgio's childhood and teenage years were also engrossed, as they are for most youths, in the rigors of study, which he always said was hard for him. God certainly has ways of bringing good out of what appears bad, and it was due to Pier Giorgio's failure in a Latin course that he would be transferred to a Jesuit school and become immersed in the Faith and in his love for Christ.

---

[203] Frassati, *A Man of the Beatitudes*, 28.
[204] Ibid., 66.

For a time Pier Giorgio pondered a priestly vocation but decided he could best use his talents to interact with and help the poor in the role of a layman. He chose the intellectually demanding field of mining engineering. The lover of mountains planned to work underneath them to improve the safety and working conditions of the poor miners whom he loved so much.

Pier Giorgio would join a variety of Catholic youth and political organizations in his teens and early twenties, all while he was also studying, going out on visits to the sick and the poor, and climbing mountains with his friends as time would permit. One group he joined was the Third Order Dominicans, and this group, of course, would demand that he grow in the love and the contemplation of God and share that contemplation with his neighbors, in his words and in his deeds. This he did like few others, in so many ways that might inspire us to do the same, until a particularly deadly strain of poliomyelitis, contracted most likely from his visits to care for the sick, brought his life to an early close at the age of twenty-four.

Let's sample now the amazing abundance of spiritual fruits that in a mere two dozen years, Pier Giorgio shared with others as a thinker, a doer, and foremost, a lover.

Contemplation from on High from an Unlikely Thinker

I call Pier Giorgio an "unlikely" thinker because of the less-than-stellar reputation as a thinker and a student that he had in his youth in the eyes of his family and in his own words. His parents, however, were unaware of just how high his thoughts reached and that his own self-descriptions of less-than-average intelligence were born of a greater-than-average humility.

Luciana wrote that her brother as a child found learning to write "a nightmare," although that was because "he could not easily write what he did not feel."[205] Pier Giorgio and Luciana both failed public examinations in 1908. Five years later, Pier Giorgio failed Latin at age twelve, which prompted his move to the private school run by the Jesuit Order. His parents considered him of limited intellect because of his academic difficulties, as well as his interests in simple pastimes such as billiards.[206] Luciana would later write of her father and brother as follows: "Branding him a simpleton, our father experienced the mysterious bafflement the man of the world feels when confronted with unworldliness."[207]

Karl Rahner, the renowned theologian, knew Pier Giorgio from a time in their youths when Pier Giorgio was a guest in his father's house in Germany, and he described the young man who impressed him so much with his sanctity and love for the poor as a man of "normal" intelligence. Pier Giorgio took on the difficult subject matter of engineering as a university student, and he managed to pass exam after exam. His letters often tell friends of his scores, often expressing relief by squeaking by with

---

[205] Frassati, *A Man of the Beatitudes*, 26. Thankfully, Pier Giorgio did come to feel the need to write letters. Hundreds of his letters exist to this day and provide wonderful insights into the heart and soul of this blessed young man. See *Pier Giorgio Frassati: Letters to His Friends and Family* (Staten, Island, NY: Alba House, 2009).

[206] Some of his letters detail negotiations with a person who was to refurbish a billiard table considered valuable by Pier Giorgio because it attracted Catholic youth to an organization where they could enjoy each other's company while growing in the Faith.

[207] Frassati, *A Man of the Beatitudes*, 39.

scores in the 60s and 70s, but sometimes expressing elation at having achieved a 90!

We, of course, are not so much interested in this young man's powers as an academic. What is so striking about Blessed Pier Giorgio Frassati is that a man of normal intelligence could ascend to such lofty heights in his contemplation of the highest things, the things of God, that is.

This chapter's opening quotation highlights his ability to see God's reflected glory in the wonder of creation laid out for him from the mountaintops in a way that would make Saint Paul (and Saints Albert and Thomas) smile. In addition to this innate sense of appreciation for God's majesty and generosity as displayed in the world, Pier Giorgio also strove to grow in his understanding of the truths revealed through the Catholic Faith. As did Saint Dominic seven hundred years before him, Pier Giorgio would come to study with particular diligence the writings of Saint Paul and the Gospel of Saint Matthew. The letters of his early adulthood reveal as well the impact he felt from the *Confessions* of Saint Augustine, and indeed, in three of the letters contained in the collection I have read, Pier Giorgio speaks of his great admiration for Saint Thomas Aquinas as he began to climb the theological mountain of the *Summa Theologica*.

It seems that virtually everything Pier Giorgio contemplated, whether secular or divine, was studied with an eye toward sharing its fruits with others, for Pier Giorgio is known and loved most as a doer — and a lover.

Doing Unto Others

Saint John Paul II would call Blessed Pier Giorgio "a man of the beatitudes," and one of the Beatitudes that blossomed early in

Pier Giorgio's life was poverty of spirit. Although he was born into a life of wealth, he never cherished material things, and his heart and his hands went out to those who were truly in need. His sister reports that when he was a very young child, a poor woman came to the door of their house carrying a child without shoes. Young Pier Giorgio quickly took off his own socks and shoes, gave them to the poor child, and slammed the door shut so no one in the house would stop him! Luciana would report that by the age of eleven, her brother had become increasingly aware of the prevalence of poverty and began to do what he could to alleviate it by collecting things such as silver paper, tram tickets, and stamps for missionaries and giving away whatever small gifts of money family members would give him.

Pier Giorgio would not cease to perform those little acts of selfless kindness for the poor for the remainder of his life, but as he reached his late teens and early twenties, he also did what he could as a doer on a broad scale, joining and actively participating in religious and political organizations, not the least of which would be the Third Order Dominicans!

He became involved in the Italian Catholic Youth Society[208] and in the Federation of Catholic University Students (FUCI). The first group consisted of mostly peasants and workers, and the second consisted mostly of the children of the wealthy. Pier Giorgio, the son of a rich father, with a heart that belonged to the poor, strove without success to fuse these two groups and unite them in a common cause. In a time and a nation fraught with conflicts between social classes, and between Church and state, Pier Giorgio had taken to heart Pope Leo XIII's call for "revolutionary change" in his 1891 encyclical *Rerum Novarum*,

---

[208] Later to become a part of the group called Catholic Action.

which championed the rights of workers to negotiate for dignified working conditions and living wages, while balancing them with the rights and the duties of property owners. Pier Giorgio particularly championed agrarian reform in restoring land to those who farmed it, believing it unjust for a relatively few landholders, including his own father, to own such vast expanses of lands that provided such meager sustenance to those who with their own hands had produced the produce.

In 1917 Pier Giorgio marched in Rome with fifty thousand youths in the fiftieth-anniversary celebration of the founding of Catholic Youth. A group of Italian royal guards including mounted cavalry charged the group and attempted to disperse them and to confiscate the flags they were carrying. The group with Pier Giorgio resisted bravely, grabbing and relentlessly holding the flag that a guard had wrenched from the standard-bearer. When a companion was threatened with a bayonet to give up his flag, Pier Giorgio ran to the officer of the guards and at the top of his lungs shouted the name of his father. Upon hearing the name of the ambassador, the officer rebuked the soldier and politely asked Pier Giorgio to leave. Pier Giorgio refused, though, and would not leave the company of his friends who had been assaulted. Luciana reported that he took up the Catholic Youth banner in one hand and his rosary in the other and invited the group to pray, "for us and for those who have hit us."[209]

The year 1922 was monumental for Pier Giorgio, and for all the people of Italy, with a blessed event on May 22 and a diabolical one on October 28. The first would set Pier Giorgio's heart on fire, and the second would, in his own words, make his blood boil.

[209] Frassati, *A Man of the Beatitudes*, 79.

On May 22, 1922, Pier Giorgio would add the initials T.O.S.D. to his name and change it to Fra Gerolamo. T.O.S.D. stands for Third Order of Saint Dominic, and Fra Gerolamo was the name he chose for himself within the order, the first name of the controversial Dominican martyr Savonarola (1452–1498). He described himself as a fervent admirer of that friar, who had fought boldly against spiritual and political corruption and ended up burned at the stake. Pier Giorgio's choice of lay orders and of his spiritual namesake revealed that by age twenty-one he was ready to preach Christ's good news and to give his very life to do so, if need be.

On October 28, 1922, Pier Giorgio would no longer be the son of the ambassador, for that is the day when Benito Mussolini and his Fascist Party came to power and the day that Alfredo Frassati resigned his ambassadorship to Germany. Pier Giorgio would write a few weeks later that his "blood boiled" when he glanced at Mussolini's speech. He saw the violence and oppression that the Fascists brought with them. Indeed, he once fought off with his own hands a small group of young Fascists who had broken into his father's home. He foresaw, but did not live to see, the extent of the brutality a few years later when the prime minister became the dictator. As a member of Italy's Popular Party, a party of many Catholics, Pier Giorgio spoke out, and for a time resigned, when some of their leaders collaborated with Mussolini's Fascists.

Pier Giorgio was always a man of heroic virtue and uncompromised principles. He saw the need to strive to promote social change, but unlike some great political reformers espousing social justice who would make the entire world into a utopia while treating those around them with little compassion and respect,[210]

---

[210] See historian Paul Johnson's *Intellectuals: From Marx to Tolstoy to Sartre and Chomsky* (New York: Harper, 2007) for

Pier Giorgio knew that true charity begins at home and with each and every individual we meet, each person being truly our brother or sister in Christ. It is for this attitude, bathed in each and every beatitude, that Pier Giorgio is known best, so let's take a look at how this most blessed young man lived out the life of his favorite scriptural passage, one that he copied out by hand, read, and lived, Saint Paul's hymn to love (1 Cor. 13).

Greater Love Has No Man Than This

It is in his role as a lover that this young hound of the Lord barks out his preaching in words and in deeds that we'd all do well to hear—and we'd also do well to add our own voices to his chorus of barking, whether or not we're afraid to bark off key! Pier Giorgio studied so hard, was frustrated in so many desires, and died at such a young age. Read his letters, and you will relive his struggle to complete his engineering degree, only to die so close to the end. You will read of his wistful love for a young orphaned woman named Laura Hidalgo, a love that he could not proclaim to her or pursue because his parents did not deem her kind worthy of their son, and he feared such an espousal would quickly push his parents' rocky marriage over the cliff of divorce. You will read of the devastation he felt when his sister Luciana got married and left the country, leaving him alone in the house where his beloved mother and father treated each other with less and less love.

---

an interesting analysis of a dozen noteworthy examples. To breathe in the clean mountain air of a very different kind of champion of social justice, I recommend Brian Kennelly's fictionalized account *To the Heights: A Novel Based on the Life of Pier Giorgio Frassati* (Charlotte, NC: TAN Books, 2014).

Nonetheless, despite all the hardships Pier Giorgio endured, you will see that as an aunt once said of him, "He is always happy with everything."[211] Saint Thomas Aquinas wrote that joy is one of the "effects" of the virtue of charity, because it makes us happy when we are enjoined with what we love. Pier Giorgio showed that a life of thinking, doing, and loving for Christ, and especially one lived in the Dominican spirit, can be, in spite of all the heavy crosses, a yoke that is light and most joyful.

Pier Giorgio was known, for example, for his love of classical music and for his penchant for singing loudly (and usually out of tune). While his father was fond of the solemn symphonic strains of Richard Wagner, Pier Giorgio had a penchant for the joyous, boisterous operas of Giuseppe Verdi. He also had an ear for the sonorous Italian poetry of Dante, which he would often recite out loud out of doors. Indeed, neighbors would call it his "preaching."

We see this joy too in the pleasure Pier Giorgio took in using the physical body that God gave him. Dominicans are champions of Christ's Incarnation. Christ took on human flesh, and human flesh is not evil. You'll recall that Saint Dominic's earliest preaching was against the Albigensian heresy that proclaimed that the flesh was evil and only the spirit good. Pier Giorgio never hesitated to put his healthy young body to the test in helping others. Even as the ambassador's son, he would often appear at events somewhat sweaty since he preferred to ride his bike to events and save the tram fare to share with the poor.[212]

---

[211] Frassati, *A Man of the Beatitudes*, 89.

[212] He also saved money to use for charity when he would use the train for longer trips. When people would ask him why he rode third class, he said it was because there was no fourth class.

When his cherished bike was stolen one day, he merely said that he supposed someone needed it more than he did.

Few things gave Pier Giorgio more joy than the climbing of mountains. He thrived on the physical exertion, and the activity provided him fellowship with the beloved friends who climbed with him. He also derived spiritual benefits from the beautiful views of God's creation that the peaks provided, and some of their mountain trips included trips to Mass in chapels in the hills.

Saint Thomas Aquinas wrote that the love of charity is a kind of friendship, and Pier Giorgio Frassati always deeply loved his friends. His sister reports that one teacher gave him the nickname *bifronte* (two fronts or faces) because he so often turned back to the students behind him, sharing a smile and a laugh. In 1924, the year before his death, he formed a tightly knit group of friends who called themselves the *Tipi Lochsi*, which has been translated as the "Sinister Ones," "Shady Characters," and even "Swindlers and Swindlerettes." They assigned each other humorous names, Pier Giorgio himself becoming "Robespierre," the heartless leader of the French Reign of Terror, who could hardly have been more his opposite. Many of these amusing letters are still extant, often ending with tongue-in-cheek cannon salutes and even with the words "Boom! Boom! Boom!"

Pier Giorgio was, then, a wonderful example of a perfectly normal and healthy young man who loved the simple joys of life with no thought of rebelling against the generous God who provides them. He is widely recognized as a tremendous model for youth in our time, and indeed, this is why Pier Giorgio's body was transported all the way to Sydney, Australia, in 2008, so that on World Youth Day, gathered around his remains, youth from all over the world could be inspired by his story to strive to love as he did.

Pier Giorgio followed Christ's Great Commandments to love God with all his heart and to love his neighbor and self through that love of God. His love of Christ was evident from early childhood when he saw a woman with flowers headed for a chapel and gave her a rose that he insisted she give to Jesus. His devotion to Christ in the Eucharist grew when he attended the Jesuit school and received permission to receive daily Communion. Indeed, his mother worried about such piety and even asked a parish priest to ask him to tone down his devotions! His devotion to Christ lasted throughout his life. At the time of his death, a book on the life of Saint Catherine of Siena sat on his nightstand. He felt a special devotion to her because she spoke to Christ while she lived on earth.

This mystical love of Christ never failed to overflow into loving actions for the least of those Pier Giorgio came across. As a child he visited a school with his grandfather and shared soup from the same bowl with an isolated young boy with a disfiguring skin condition. As a young student, he noticed that a janitor seemed particularly forlorn one day. He asked him why and learned that the janitor's teenage son had recently died. Nearly a year later, he saw the janitor again, remembered the date of the boy's death, and told him he would pray for him that day. Many people remarked how he was always loved by the porters. He was no respecter of titles alone, but treated every person with dignity.

Pier was blessed with above average height, remarkable good looks, an athletic build, and of course, he came from a respected, wealthy, aristocratic family. He could have "hobnobbed" with whomever he preferred, but, as his sister Luciana noted, he always seemed to gravitate toward the least attractive, most discouraged member of any group. He would say he could see a "special light around the poor," a light imperceptible to most, and a light that drew him forth to the poor at night. Whether in Italy or in Germany, through organizations including the Saint Vincent de Paul Society, Pier Giorgio would venture out into the slums, befriending the sick, the poor, and the friendless, catering to their physical and spiritual needs.

Pier Giorgio did not hide his light under a bushel basket, yet ironically, most of his family would not perceive the radiance of that light and the warmth it provided for so many people until after his death. Oblivious to his son's desires, talents, and years of study in the field of engineering, in June 1925, only a month before Pier Giorgio's unexpected death, Alfredo arranged a job for him at his newspaper and, while he was gone, had an employee break the news to him and show him the office that had already been set up for him. In that same month, Pier Giorgio climbed his last mountain.

In the last days of June 1925, Pier Giorgio's beloved grandmother Linda lay on her deathbed until her soul left her body on the first of July. Pier Giorgio, just down the hall, was lying in bed as well, but everyone assumed it was just a passing illness. He drew no attention to himself, and hobbled as best he could to visit his grandmother's bedside. People had noticed that his clothing began to dangle from the once robust physique, but they had no idea that his illness would soon become terminal. Indeed, in his last days, his mother would chide him for being unable to help the family with her mother's funeral.

It was not until the day before his death that the family would realize Pier Giorgio had become paralyzed from the waist down. Once the gravity of his condition was known, his family immediately sought medical attention. The doctor determined that Pier Giorgio had contracted a rare and devastating strain of poliomyelitis. A vaccine existed that could counter the disease, although possibly not at this late stage. Further, there was none available in all of Italy. The nearest available dose was in Paris, France. When the nearness of his death was evident, Pier Giorgio wrote a note to be delivered to Giuseppe Grimaldi, a friend from the Saint Vincent de Paul Society:

> The injections are for Converso and the pawn ticket belongs to Sappa; I had forgotten it. Please renew it on my account.[213]

Even on his deathbed, Pier Giorgio's thoughts went out to others in need. The doctors concluded that his polio had probably been contracted through his interactions with the sick and the poor, but Pier Giorgio would not have had it any other way. Christ showed us and Saint John told us, "Greater love has no man than this, that a man lay down his life for his friends (John 15:13). Pier Giorgio knew this, and he did this. Can his example inspire us, even in the smallest of daily deeds, at no risk to our health or possessions, to give unto others a little of that love that Christ and Pier Giorgio sacrificed so much to give?

[213] Frassati, *A Man of the Beatitudes*, 151.

Servant of God Mother Mary Alphonsa Hawthorne

1851–1926 | FEAST: JULY 9

The hounds of the Lord come in all breeds, shapes, sizes, and colors, even in fiery redheads born to great American (and Protestant) authors. On May 20, 1851, in Lenox, Massachusetts, Rose Hawthorne was born, the second daughter of novelist Nathaniel Hawthorne[214] and his wife, Sophia. Before her father's death in 1864, the family had lived in England, France, and Italy. At the Vatican Gardens on one fateful day, young Rose almost ran headlong into Pope Pius IX, who beamed at her benevolently and blessed her as he passed. A few years later, her mother also passed away. Rose later met the writer George Lathrop. They married, moved to New York, and she gave birth to a son who died at age five. George drifted into alcohol, and their marriage drifted apart just two years after they had both become Catholic.

Not long afterward, while Rose was out of town, she learned that a seamstress who had worked for her had died of cancer in her absence, all alone in a hospital for the poor. This triggered in Rose her vocation to care for the sick and the poor. She formed a group of friends to care for dying cancer patients. A

---

[214] Nathaniel Hawthorne was the author of classics including *The Scarlet Letter* and *The House of Seven Gables*. His friend Herman Melville dedicated his epic novel *Moby Dick* to him.

Dominican took notice of her actions, and before long, after her husband's death in 1898, at which she had been at his side, Rose was persuaded on December 8, 1990, to don the Dominican habit, taking the name Mary Alphonsa. She would found the Dominican Congregation of Saint Rose of Lima, later called the Servants of Relief for Incurable Cancer. She died on July 9, 1926, her parents' wedding anniversary. Her cause for canonization opened in 2003. May this Servant of God inspire us to serve those who need us most.

CONCLUSION

Our Turn to Let the Dogs Out

*Behold, my children, the heritage I leave. Have
charity for one another, guard humility, make
your treasure out of voluntary poverty.*
—Saint Dominic de Guzman

*The Dominican Order exists in order to be useful
to other people, and it has always been prepared
to adapt its own style and behavior to fit the
requirements of those it seeks to serve.*
—Simon Tugwell, O.P., *Early Dominicans*

Today I sit behind "Colossus," my eight-foot-long writing desk
and monastic cell of sorts over the course of these last few
months. A quick glance to the right reminds me why. There
stands in resin, just half a foot or so tall, the image of a lean
and fiery man frozen in action as depicted by his furled and
flowing habit. The index finger of his right hand points upward,
directing us toward the higher things of God. In his left hand
are open Scriptures, most likely the Gospel of Saint Matthew,
or perhaps the letters of Saint Paul. Beside him stands a furry

dog, a hound of the Lord, no doubt, complete with a flaming torch in his mouth. It was the man's feast day just yesterday. For 794 years now, he has made his home in heaven. In just one more year, the family he created will have done its share toward bringing heaven to earth for a full eight hundred years.

Saint Dominic's statue serves to remind me that the legacy of Saint Dominic is alive and well today. Saint Dominic tells us to praise, bless, and preach, to contemplate God, to spread the good word of His gospel, and to share His love with our neighbor. He tells us to be thinkers, doers, and lovers for Christ. As simple and sensible as this might seem, it is not the world's message today.

We are told not to be *thinkers*, whose motto is "truth," but to be *opiners*, so to speak, entitled to express our opinions but without obligation to be sure our opinions are grounded in truth. We are told not to be *doers* who get the job done for God, but to be *spectators* who watch on glowing screens of various sizes others who get their jobs done in order to entertain us, whether or not for the glory of God (and unfortunately, often not). We are told not to be *lovers* who give, but *getters* who receive and ask ourselves about everything, "What's in it for me?"

One way to counter modern pressures to conform to the world and to ignore God is to embrace the Dominican way, that glorious way with as many unique variations as there are human souls. Surely we can draw inspiration and spiritual strength from the lives and the lessons of the great panoply of Dominican saints, from the intellectual giants, to the enrapt mystics, to the men and the women who scrubbed the floors or who cared for the dying. I hope this book has whetted your appetite to dig deeper into the lives and lessons of these and other saints and blesseds who lived in the joyous Dominican way.

The hounds of the Lord are still out there, roaming the world, seeking out souls to retrieve for Christ, from the friars, both priests and religious brothers, to cloistered contemplative nuns, to sisters engaged in the active life of teaching and healing, to lay Dominicans of every walk of life. We can do what we can to support their efforts and do what we can to be like them, as they strive to be like Christ.

Inspired by the stories of their saints and armed with their saintly intercession, it is time to be jubilant with them as they celebrate the Jubilee of their first eight hundred years. It is also our turn to let the dogs out, to see God more clearly, love him more dearly, and follow him more nearly, as we share the fruits we have gathered by contemplating the words and deeds of these holy hounds of the Lord.

A Chronology of Some
Saintly Dominicans

(Based on approximate date of birth. Many of the earlier dates are uncertain and may vary in other sources.)

Saint Dominic de Guzman (1170–1221)

Blessed Reginald of Orléans (1183–1220)

Saint Hyacinth of Poland (1185–1257)

Blessed Jordan of Saxony (1190–1237)

Blessed Humbert of Romans (1193–1277)

Saint Richard of Chichester (1197–1253)

Saint Albert the Great (1200–1280)

Blessed Cecilia Caesarini (1200–1290)

Blessed Diana d'Andalo (1201–1236)

Saint Peter of Verona, aka Saint Peter Martyr (1206–1252)

Saint Thomas Aquinas (1225–1274)

Pope Saint Innocent V (1225–1276)

Saint Agnes of Montepulciano (1268–1317)

Blessed Henry Suso (1290–1365)

Saint Catherine of Siena (1347–1380)

Saint Vincent Ferrer (1350–1419)

Saint Antoninus (1289–1459)

Blessed Fra Angelico (1395–1455)

Pope Saint Pius V (1504–1572)
Venerable Louis of Granada (1505–1588)
Saint Catherine de Ricci (1522–1589)
Bishop Bartolome de la Casas (1484–1546)
Saint Martin de Porres (1579–1639)
Saint Juan (John) Macias (1585–1645)
Saint Rose of Lima (1586–1617)
Saint Louis de Montfort (1673–1716)
Mother Alphonsa Hawthorne (1851–1926)
Blessed Pier Giorgio Frassati (1901–1925)

A Partial Calendar of Dominican Feasts

January 3	Blessed Henry Suso
January 28	Saint Thomas Aquinas
February 12	Blessed Reginald of Orleans
February 13	Blessed Jordan of Saxony and Saint Catherine di Ricci
February 18	Blessed Fra Angelico
April 3	Saint Richard of Chichester
April 5	Saint Vincent Ferrer
April 20	Saint Agnes of Montepulciano
April 28	Saint Louis de Montfort
April 29	Saint Catherine of Siena, Saint Peter of Verona
April 30	Pope Saint Pius V
June 8	Blessed Diana d'Andalo and Blessed Cecilia Caesarini
June 22	Pope Saint Innocent V
July 4	Blessed Pier Giorgio Frassati
July 9	Mother Mary Alphonsa Hawthorne
July 14	Blessed Humbert of Romans
July 30	Blessed Mannes de Guzman
August 2	Blessed Jane of Aza
August 8	Saint Dominic de Guzman

August 17	Saint Hyacinth of Poland
August 23	Saint Rose of Lima
September 18	Saint Juan (John) Macias
November 3	Saint Martin de Porres
November 15	Saint Albert the Great
December 22	Anniversary of Pope Honorius III's approval of the order
December 31	Venerable Louis of Granada

ABOUT THE AUTHOR
Kevin Vost

Kevin Vost (b. 1961) holds a Doctor of Psychology in Clinical Psychology (Psy.D.) degree from the Adler School of Professional Psychology in Chicago. He has taught at Aquinas College in Nashville, the University of Illinois at Springfield, MacMurray College, and Lincoln Land Community College. He has served as a research review committee member for American Mensa, a society promoting the scientific study of human intelligence, and as an advisory board member for the International Association of Resistance Trainers, an organization that certifies personal fitness trainers. Dr. Vost drinks great drafts of coffee while studying timeless, Thomistic tomes in the company of his wife, two sons, and their two dogs, in Springfield, Illinois.

Sophia Institute

Sophia Institute is a nonprofit institution that seeks to nurture the spiritual, moral, and cultural life of souls and to spread the Gospel of Christ in conformity with the authentic teachings of the Roman Catholic Church.

Sophia Institute Press fulfills this mission by offering translations, reprints, and new publications that afford readers a rich source of the enduring wisdom of mankind.

Sophia Institute also operates two popular online Catholic resources: CrisisMagazine.com and CatholicExchange.com.

Crisis Magazine provides insightful cultural analysis that arms readers with the arguments necessary for navigating the ideological and theological minefields of the day. *Catholic Exchange* provides world news from a Catholic perspective as well as daily devotionals and articles that will help you to grow in holiness and live a life consistent with the teachings of the Church.

In 2013, Sophia Institute launched Sophia Institute for Teachers to renew and rebuild Catholic culture through service to Catholic education. With the goal of nurturing the spiritual, moral, and cultural life of souls, and an abiding respect for the role and work of teachers, we strive to provide materials and programs that are at once enlightening to the mind and ennobling to the heart; faithful and complete, as well as useful and practical.

Sophia Institute gratefully recognizes the Solidarity Association for preserving and encouraging the growth of our apostolate over the course of many years. Without their generous and timely support, this book would not be in your hands.

www.SophiaInstitute.com
www.CatholicExchange.com
www.CrisisMagazine.com
www.SophiaInstituteforTeachers.org

Sophia Institute Press® is a registered trademark of Sophia Institute.
Sophia Institute is a tax-exempt institution as defined by the
Internal Revenue Code, Section 501(c)(3). Tax I.D. 22-2548708.